No one will dispute that one of the most pressing problems of this day is how to handle children vis-a-vis the TV set.

The average child spends more hours watching television than doing any other activity except sleeping—roughly some 54 hours each week.

What can the parent do about this?

What should the parent do about this?

This book provides some very good answers.

HOW TO RAISE CHILDREN IN A TV WORLD

Dr. Leland W. Howe
Temple University

Dr. Bernard Solomon
Philadelphia Public Schools

Illustrated by Beverly Muschlitz

HART PUBLISHING COMPANY, INC.
New York

To my parents, who provided the foundation for my own parenting.

—Leland W. Howe

To my wife, Lesley, and to our loving sons, Eric and Danny. Also, to my mother.

—Bernard Solomon

ACKNOWLEDGEMENTS

I wish to acknowledge the support and guidance graciously given by Dr. Michael P. Marcase, Superintendent of the School District of Philadelphia. Dr. Marcase, as a co-creator of the Television Reading Program concept, was the single person most responsible for the concept's viability. His genius is unsurpassed and is also demonstrated in the higher achievement of the district's children. Also, the Parent Partnership Program, another important creation by Dr. Marcase, has brought huge numbers of parents into the learning process of their children.

Additionally, I would like to acknowledge Michael McAndrew as a creative co-founder of the Television Reading Program, and of the program's many applications. —Bernard Solomon

I wish to acknowledge Mary Martha Howe for her contribution of many suggestions and additions which greatly improved the manuscript of my book. I also wish to thank Margaret Hazzard for her careful work in preparing and typing the manuscript. Appreciation must also be extended to my children, Liesl, Peter, and Toryn, without whom I would have been unable to develop and field-test many of the ideas in this book. —Leland W. Howe

CONTENTS

Introduction: TV or No TV?:
That is the Question (Or is it?)   9

**Part I: How to Deal with the Negative Effects of
Television on Your Child**   15

1. Introduction to Part I   17
2. How to Tame the "One-Eyed Monster"   23
3. How to Deal with TV Violence   39
4. How to Deal with Kidvid Commercials   47
5. How to Help Your Child
   Kick the TV Habit   55
6. How to Deal with Your Child's
   TV-Related Emotional Upsets   67
7. How to Influence
   Television Programming   77

**Part II: How to Make Television a Positive
Experience for Your Child**   87

8. Introduction to Part II   89
9. How to Use TV to Increase Your
   Child's Learning Power   93
10. How to Use TV to Nurture Your
    Child's Values and Moral Development   113

11. How to Answer Your Child's
     TV Questions   147

12. How to Use Television in the
     Classroom: A Guide for
     Teachers and Parents   159

13. How to Use TV as a Creative
     Babysitter Without Feeling Guilty   175

**Part III: How to Prepare Your Child to
Live in a TV World**   181

14. Introduction to Part III   183

15. Family Time: Value-Clarification
     Activities to Prepare Your Child
     for a TV World   189

16. Special Time: Self-esteem Activities to
     Prepare Your Child for a TV World   233

Selected Annotated Bibliography   257

Index   261

INTRODUCTION
TV OR NO TV?:
THAT IS THE
QUESTION(OR IS IT?)

Consider the following facts:

—The average child today spends more hours watching television than doing any other activity except sleeping.[1]

—The average pre-school child today watches more than 54 hours of TV each week—an average of almost eight hours of TV-viewing per day.[2]

—By the time he or she graduates from high school, the average teenager will spend almost twice as much time before the television set than in the classroom.[3]

—At midnight on any evening, there are over two million children between the ages of two and eleven still glued to the TV set.[4]

—By the age of 15, today's average teenager has witnessed between 11,000 and 13,000 acts of violence on television.[5]

The debate over the effects of television upon our children and upon the family has been going on now for more than 30 years. Television has been the subject of congressional hearings, a presidentially-appointed study commission, and hundreds of newspaper and magazine editorials and articles. Debate has most often focused on the question, "TV or no TV?" The TV critics have deplored the enormity of television violence, the banality of most television programs, and the insidious, materialistic brainwashing of television commercials; many TV critics have called for an outright ban on television viewing. The TV advocates—primarily the television networks and sponsors—have defended the status quo, issuing statements and reports contending that children and families are not adversely affected by television.

Unfortunately, much of the debate has consisted of opinion in the guise of authority, with no factually-based understanding of television's impact upon people. Recently, however, two books about television, backed by comprehensive research, have been published. The books are *Remote Control*[6] by Frank Mankiewicz and Joel Swerdlow and *The Plug-In Drug*[7] by Marie Winn. Both books attempt to assess television's impact upon children, families, and social institutions. *Remote Control: Television and the Manipulation of American Life* is by far the more comprehensive of the two books. On the subject of television violence alone, Mankiewicz and Swerdlow contend that they have read "virtually *all* the scientific studies" on the question of television violence and its relationship to violence in American homes and streets. Their analysis of television and its effects upon race relations, sex roles, and learning, as well as on many other areas of American life, is equally informed. Here are the conclusions that we reached after reading *Remote Control:*

1. Television is here to stay.

Anyone who seriously believes that parents or anyone else (with the exception of a few individuals and families) will simply pull the plug as a means of effectively dealing with the problems created by television is not facing reality.

2. Television has an enormous impact upon our children, families, and social institutions.

TV teaches values, alters family routines and relationships, determines what is newsworthy and what is not, affects political behavior, and acts upon us in many other ways.

3. The current impact of television upon children, families, and society is mostly negative.

TV increases violent behavior in both children and adults; is the leading cause of the national decline in reading scores; teaches both young and old that happiness is dependent upon using the right soap, deodorant, and toothpaste, and upon owning the right car; and creates an unfounded fear that crime is much more extensive in most communities than it really is. And this is just for starters.

4.   Television can have a positive effect upon children, families, and social institutions—if it is used judiciously.

For example, *Mister Rodgers Neighborhood* teaches children to empathize with others, to value inner qualities rather than the appearance of individuals, to help friends, and to deal with their own fears. The program is widely acclaimed by educators and child specialists as one of the most positive and beneficial children's shows on TV. The Philadelphia Schools' TV Reading Project uses television scripts in conjunction with videotaped programs to dramatically increase children's reading abilities, and Chicago's Prime Time School Television, a non-profit organization, uses popular television programs as a basis for classroom instruction on interpreting news, clarifying values, analyzing advertising, and understanding politics and economics. Both projects are regarded by educators as successful and beneficial.

5.   The major factor in determining the positive or negative impact of television on children is parental intervention (or intervention from other adults, such as teachers, grandparents, or older brothers and sisters).

Studies show that when parents view TV programs along with their children, and talk with their children about what they are viewing, the children are likely to gain more skills and a better understanding of the various concepts presented than when left alone before the TV screen. Similarly, when parents watch even the most violent TV programs with their adolescent off-spring, and then discuss the alternatives to such violent modes of problem-solving, the adolescents are often induced to adopt pro-social behavior rather than the violent behavior promoted by TV.

After reviewing the facts, it would seem to us, that the old formulation of the question, "TV or no TV?" misses the point. Rather, the question should be, "How can television be used to nurture, promote, and bring out the best in our children, families, and social institutions?" If parents, educators, and child specialists were to demand that both the television advocates and TV critics address themselves to this question, we might see some immediate, positive changes in television programming, management, and viewing.

PART I

HOW TO DEAL WITH THE NEGATIVE EFFECTS OF TELEVISION ON YOUR CHILD

1 INTRODUCTION TO PART I

INTRODUCTION TO PART I

Consider the following:

—The National Commission on the Causes and Prevention of Violence, appointed by President Johnson in 1968, concluded in its report that, "Television enters powerfully into the learning process of children and teaches them a set of moral and social values about violence which are inconsistent with the standards of a civilized society."[1]

—The National Child Research Center reported to the FCC in 1971 that, "Television represses children's innate tendencies because it requires passive rather than active involvement, and activity—not passivity—is necessary for children's full healthful development."[2]

—In 1976, television advertisers spent more than $400 million for commercials designed to sell our children an avalanche of sugary glop and fad toys. Several public interest groups charge that, "Television is creating a nation of sugar junkies."[3]

Television reform may be coming slowly, as many parent and professional activist groups put pressure on the networks and the federal government to do something about the situation. However, as a parent, you do not have to wait until reform comes—if it comes at all. There are things you can do *now* to protect your child from the negative effects of television. Each of the chapters in this section presents numerous tested methods of dealing with the various child-raising problems created by television. We have included a chapter on how to set limits on TV viewing and how to solve the TV battle; a chapter on dealing with TV violence; a chapter on how to cope with TV advertising; a chapter on helping your child kick the TV habit; a chapter on how to handle your child's TV-related emotional upsets, and a chapter on how to influence television programming.

THE PURPOSE AND ORGANIZATION OF THIS BOOK

The purpose of this book is not to discuss or evaluate the effects of television on our children. Mankiewicz, Swerdlow, and Winn have already done a superb job of this in their respective books, *Remote Control* and *The Plug-In Drug;* we see no need to duplicate their successful efforts. Instead, we will focus on the question, "How can we, as parents and teachers, use television to bring out the best in our children?" We will suggest many field-tested and practical ways to use television positively and constructively in the home and school to promote child development and to deal effectively with the problems that television creates.

This book is divided into three parts. Part I focuses on ways to minimize the negative effects of TV on children. This section contains six chapters, which address such problems as how to deal effectively with television addiction, violence, and commercials; how to set limits on TV viewing; how to deal with your child's TV questions and emotional upsets; and how to influence television programming. Part II focuses on ways to maximize the positive effects of TV on children. This section contains five chapters, which deal with such questions as how to use television to increase your child's learning power and nurture your child's values development; how TV can be used in the classroom; and how to use TV as a creative babysitter. Part III focuses on ways to prepare children to live in a television-oriented and dominated society. This section contains two chapters, one of which addresses the subject of helping your child to develop strong, clear values, and the other focuses on your child's development of a positive self-image. Both factors are crucial for any child who must deal with a world of mass communication and rapid change.

HOW TO USE THIS BOOK

We have designed this book so that it can be used by parents, teachers, and child specialists—in short, by anyone who works with or is involved in raising children. Some chapters, like "How To Tame The One-Eyed Monster," are more appropriate for parent use, while other chapters, like "How To Nurture Your Child's Value and Moral Development," have both homeand school applications. In these chapters, the teacher or child-specialist need only change the reference to parents so that it applies to his or her own situation. Thus, an activity which the parent might use in the home on an individual or "family small group" basis can be used in the school in the same way. Chapter 12, "Using Television In The Classroom," is designed specifically for teachers, counselors, and parents who work in a classroom setting, and will provide many ideas and suggestions on how activities in other chapters can be used on a class basis.

We have written about ideas and activities which have worked for us and for many other parents and teachers. However, you should feel free to adapt these ideas and activities, or to change them to fit your children's and your own personalities and circumstances. You know best what will work for you and your children.

We wish you success in using the ideas and activities in this book, and we hope that they prove as effective in dealing with television in your family as they have in ours.

Footnotes

[1]Mankiewicz, Frank and Joel Swerdlow, *Remote Control*, Times Books, New York, 1978.
[2]Association for Childhood Education International, *Children and TV*, Washington, D.C., 1967
[3]Walters, Harry F., "What TV Does To Kids," *Newsweek*, February 21, 1977.

2 HOW TO TAME THE "ONE-EYED MONSTER"

HOW TO TAME THE "ONE-EYED MONSTER"

The TV set can become a "one-eyed monster" when children want to watch it every waking minute, constantly fight over which programs to watch, clamor for every toy that is advertised, and imitate the violent behavior that they see on TV. Fortunately, however, there are some effective ways to tame the monster. Here are the ways we use and recommend.

1. Start TV training early.

If your child is under three years of age, start regulating his or her TV viewing now. With your spouse, agree upon which programs your pre-schoolers can watch each day. Then, stick to your guns. One way to decide which programs are appropriate for your child is to think about what character traits you want to foster in your child, and then to choose TV programs which promote such traits. For example, if you want your child to learn to help others, then *Mister Rodgers Neighborhood* would be an excellent choice. If you are undecided about a show, watch several episodes to determine whether the show promotes positive values, like helping others, thinking things through before acting, and solving problems non-violently, or negative values like racism and sexism, violence, and passivity.

In our family, we let our pre-schoolers watch *Mister Rodgers Neighborhood* and *Zoom* on a regular basis, because these programs encourage children to cooperate with and help others, as well as to use their imaginations creatively; these are values traits which we want our children to develop. Occasionally, our pre-schoolers are allowed to stay up past bedtime so that our whole family can view an episode of *The Waltons* or of *The Little House on the Prairie*. These two programs promote cooperation in the family, helping others, and using non-violent ways to solve problems—all very important character traits which we want our children to develop.

2. Avoid the tempting habit of using the TV to babysit for your pre-schoolers.

That's when you begin to lose control. It is easier said than done, especially between the hours of 4:30 and 6:00 p.m., when you are trying to get dinner, answer the phone, finish the laundry, and keep your pre-schoolers from tearing the house apart; however, some forethought on how to keep your pre-schoolers occupied at this or any other hectic time of the day can help you keep from turning on the TV as a means of maintaining your sanity. Make a list of things that you can do to keep your pre-schoolers occupied. For example:

—Getting them set up at the kitchen table, where they can still be near you, with coloring books and crayons or an art project.
—Suggesting an imaginative game such as school,

store, ship, etc., which they can play in their rooms with dress-up clothes.

—Getting a toy that they have not played with for a while and inducing them to play with it.

—Letting them help you cook by measuring, pouring, and so on (if you have a lot of patience).

—Sending them outside with a play suggestion.

Then, post the list somewhere handy, such as the refrigerator door, so that you can easily refer to the list when things get out of hand.

3. Help your children to develop a healthy attitude toward TV.

One way to do this is to share your views on TV watching. For example, you might explain to your children that you realize TV viewing is fun, but that there are lots of better ways to use time. If your children have trouble thinking of any better ways, sit down with them and help them make a list. Then post the list for future reference.

4. Don't get pulverized by the "It isn't fair routine."

One of the major arguments our children use on us goes like this, "But it isn't fair! At Joey's house we get to watch any program we want!" Stay rational and explain that each family has different rules and ways of doing things in their homes; that "in our home, TV viewing is limited to two programs a day," or whatever; that, "when you are at Joey's house, you live by Joey's family's rules and you can watch TV as much as you want, but in our home we have decided there are better ways to use our time." There is no need to put Joey's family down as having the wrong views; just point out that there are differences in the way each family does things. Persist with this strategy and it will work. Children readily accept differences which they see for themselves exist among families; but to get their way, they will often resort to the "it isn't fair" routine.

5. Use no-lose problem-solving to work out television-related conflicts and disagreements.

No-lose solutions are very effective, since their intent is to have everyone involved in the conflict win. This doesn't mean that each person gets just exactly what he or she wants, but the solution to the disagreement leaves everyone feeling good about the outcome. Thus, there is a subtle but important difference between a compromise solution and a no-lose solution. In a compromise solution, each person gives up something to get something; the feeling that one has to give up part of what he or she wants in order to get the other part often produces negative feelings which can later undermine the compromise. In no-lose problem-solving, the solution to the disagreement may be far different from what each person originally wanted, but it leaves each person feeling that he or she is the winner. This kind of solution is likely to be a solid and permanent solution, since everyone involved is pleased with the outcome. Of course, no-lose problem-solving takes more time to work out initially than compromise, but it is often well worth the extra time. The problem stays solved and there are few, if any, negative side- or after-effects.

To use no-lose problem-solving, follow these steps. (Remember, respect for each person's feelings and thinking is the most important key to making no-lose problem-solving work.)

STEPS IN USING NO-LOSE PROBLEM-SOLVING

Step 1: Each person makes a statement of his or her needs in relation to the problem.

Step 2: After each person makes his or her needs statement, the other person repeats back his or her understanding of the other person's needs until a clear understanding is achieved.

Step 3: Once the problem of disagreement and each person's needs are fully understood, those involved list as many possible solutions to the problem or disagreement as they can think of, even solutions that seem way-out and unrealistic, for these may trigger good alternatives. No evaluation of alternatives is permitted at this point.

Step 4: When all the possible solutions have been listed, the unrealistic solutions are then crossed out, and attention is turned to identifying the consequences and outcomes of each solution. Both pros and cons should be noted.

Step 5: Finally, those involved evaluate the solutions and try to agree upon a solution that is mutually acceptable, and thus meets everyone's needs. If this is not possible, the persons involved should go back and repeat steps 1-5 until a mutually agreeable solution is found.

Let me provide an example of how we used no-lose problem-solving in our family. My oldest daughter was getting into the habit of watching TV more than my wife and I thought wise. We were very busy at the time, and just let the situation slide for awhile. When we began to take steps to correct the situation, we encountered a good deal of resistance. Of course, we could simply have put our foot down and said "no" to the TV watching, but we were well aware of the price we would pay for issuing an ultimatum. Our daughter has a mind of her own, and we knew that she would find at least a dozen ways to remind us of that fact if we used our power.

Instead, we held a family meeting and went through the above problem-solving procedure. First, we parents stated our concern that our daughter was watching too much television, which we thought was not good for her social and intellectual development, and which we felt was also interfering with our family activities. We stated that we had a need to feel that we were doing the best job we could do as parents, as well as a need to have more family-centered time. When it was her turn, our daughter said that there were several programs which she really wanted to be able to watch. Upon further discussion, it became evident that her major need was to have some control over which programs she was allowed to watch.

Next, we turned our attention to solving the problem. We brainstormed, and then were able to agree upon some criteria for which shows our daughter could watch. The major criteria were that the programs 1) had to be free of violence, sexism, and "put-downs" 2) would encourage such positive values as helping others, solving problems non-violently, and appreciating others for their inner qualities rather than for their appearance, and 3) would encourage active involvement (using imagination, making and building things, creative movement, problem-solving, etc.) rather than simply passive viewing. We then made a list of all the programs which met these criteria.

As for the amount of viewing time, we composed a list ranging from two programs a week to an unlimited amount of TV viewing time. After a good deal of discussion about how our daughter should spend her leisure time each week, we agreed that ten hours of TV each week was about right, unless there were any special programs that week. This left our daughter in control of her choice of shows (as long as the programs met the previously agreed upon criteria) and when she wanted to watch TV. The problem was solved, and everyone emerged from the discussion feeling like the winner.

6. If no-lose problem-solving fails, use natural or logical consequences.

No-lose problem-solving works well with older children who are willing to enter into discussion and play by the rules. It does not work very well with younger children, who are unable to reason effectively as yet, or with older children who have such a battle going with their parents that they will sabotage the no-lose approach as a means of retaliation. Natural or logical consequences can be used in these situations with great effectiveness. Not only can natural or logical consequences be used to solve many family conflicts, this approach is also an excellent "teacher." Let's explore a familiar incident to see how the approach works.

Two-year-old Betty is approaching a hot radiator. Her mother tells her, "No! The radiator is hot, Betty. You'll be burned if you touch it." Betty ignores the warning, and starts for the radiator again. Her mother rushes over and gives Betty a sharp swat on her behind, with the words, "I said *no!*" Now, this is not an example of natural consequences. The natural consequence of Betty's touching the radiator is not a swat on the bottom. Betty does not connect the swat on the bottom with the hot radiator. She does learn, however, that she will get a spanking if she goes near the radiator, so she will stay away from it for awhile. However, in a short time, or with a different radiator, she will try again. Betty's mother will again have to administer a swat on the bottom to keep Betty away from the radiator. And so it goes—the battle between mother and child is on.

The natural consequence of Betty touching the hot radiator is that she will get burned. Naturally, this is not a pleasant experience for the child, but she will learn very quickly not to touch hot things—it usually only takes one burning. Thus, if Betty's mother decides to stop protecting Betty and to let her experience the consequences of her behavior (getting burned when she touches the hot radiator), she will quickly accomplish two objectives. One, she will avoid the power struggle which in the long run can have a much more damaging effect on both Betty and her relationship with her mother, and two, Betty learns a valuable lesson—not to touch hot things.

Of course, the use of natural consequences must necessarily be limited to behavior which does not produce disastrous consequences. For example, no parent would think of allowing a two-year-old child to run in the road and experience the consequences of his or her behavior. The result of such an experiment could be death or serious injury. In this kind of situation, *logical* consequences can be used.

For example, I told my three-year-old daughter that she was not allowed to play in or near the street. Five minutes later, she was headed toward the street. I picked her up without any show of emotion, and took her to the house. "I'm sorry," I said. "It is very dangerous near the street; therefore, the rule is, that when outside you must play in the back yard and not go near the street. If you can not follow the rules of playing outside, then you will have to play inside today. Tomorrow, we will try it again, and if you can play in the back yard and not go near the street, then you can stay outside." The next day I did the same thing. It took exactly three times of returning my daughter to the house when she went into the front yard to convince her that I meant what I said. From then on, she played in the back yard. My daughter simply learned that the logical consequence of going to the front of the house was that she could not play outside.

Logical consequences work only if the child does not view the consequence "imposed" as a punishment. By showing no emotion and explaining why I couldn't allow my daughter to go near the street, I acted very rationally and logically. My daughter responded by simply accepting the back yard as the natural boundary of her play-world outside. Had I got angry or spanked her as I took her into the house, the situation would have been very different. Such behavior would have precipitated a power struggle, which could eventually have led to a disastrous outcome.

Natural and logical consequences can readily be applied to the TV battle. For example, at one point I was having trouble getting my daughter to the dinner table on time, because she wanted to continue watching TV. My inclination was to threaten her, or to simply go in and turn off the TV set. In either case, my daughter would probably have come to dinner with a pout on her face, resenting me for using force to get my way. Instead, I restrained myself, and simply told her that dinner was ready. Nothing else. No threats! No anger! Nothing except, "Come to dinner."

Then the rest of the family sat down to dinner. When we finished eating, we cleared the table and put the food away. When my daughter finished her program and came to the table to eat, I simply explained to her that dinner was over. She experienced the logical consequence of her choice. No amount of begging, anger, etc., got her her way. Nor did I get angry or upset. Also, she was not allowed to eat between meals, because this would destroy the effectiveness of using logical consequences. This may sound harsh, allowing my daughter to go hungry for a meal or two, but it was much less damaging to my daughter and to our relationship than forcing her to come to the dinner table and then having to deal with her resentment.

Actually, what I did in this situation was to follow up the logical consequences approach with a no-lose problem-solving session. The outcome in our family was that we agreed to have dinner a half-hour later, so that my daughter could watch her favorite TV program, *zoom*. If I were to do it over again, I would try no-lose problem-solving first, and if this failed, use logical consequences.

Let's take another familiar problem and see how logical consequences can be used to provide a solution. Let's suppose that my children are not doing their chores after school (taking out the trash, sweeping the kitchen, etc.) but instead, flip on the TV. Instead of getting angry at them, I simply leave the kitchen one night, and work on another project until dinner. About six o'clock, the children begin to ask about dinner. I explain that I can't work in a kitchen where the trash piles up, the floor is not swept, etc., and therefore I cannot cook dinner. However, when the trash is taken out, the floor swept, and so on, I will be glad to fix dinner. I do not get angry, but simply explain this in a very rational way. Let me testify that this particular use of logical consequences works, and works very effectively. (For more on the use of natural and logical consequences, see Rudolf Dreikurs's *Children, the Challenge*, Hawthorne, New York, 1964.)

7. Suggest alternatives to TV.

This method of solving the TV battle is so simple that we often overlook it. For example, many children watch much more TV than we would like for the simple reason that they feel that there is nothing more exciting to do. This situation can be changed by helping them come up with some ideas for having fun without TV. One way to do this is to have each child make a list of things that he or she really likes to do. If your child is too young to write, have him or her call out the activities, and *you* write the list. Give the children a goal to shoot for, like, "See if you can think of 20 things you like to do." Many children can think of 50 or more things to do, if encouraged. Then, help the children begin to make plans to do some of the things on their list. This can cut TV viewing to a minimum. Another antidote to too much TV viewing is to use the TV program as a stimulus for further play. For example, my seven-year-old daughter loves *The Little House On The Prairie*. One morning, I suggested that she use wooden blocks to outline a cabin and play *Little House On The Prairie*. My daughter spent over three hours constructing the cabin and replaying her own version of the episode that she had viewed the previous night.

8. Last but not least, set the example for the behavior you want your children to adopt.

For instance, if you want your children to limit their TV viewing, then cut back on yours. Sitting in front of the TV set all weekend watching the sports spectacular, and then telling your children that too much TV is not good for them rings hollow. You do not practice what you preach—and neither will they.

Remember, too, that "an ounce of prevention is worth a pound of cure." Don't use television as a babysitter for infants and then expect them to kick the TV habit when they get older. Right from infancy, encourage your children to form active interests and plan family activities that are not TV-centered. Then, as your children get older, they may find other activities more stimulating and challenging than watching TV.

3 HOW TO DEAL WITH TV VIOLENCE

HOW TO DEAL WITH TV VIOLENCE

After 25 years of research and 2,300 studies and reports on the subject, including 50 comprehensive studies involving 10,000 children from every possible background, researchers have concluded that viewing television violence tends to produce aggressive behavior among children.[1] In a very recent study, evidence was uncovered that TV violence also increases children's tolerance of violent behavior in others.[2] For many parents and organizations, the debate over the effects of TV violence is finished. They are taking action to end the violence. For example, the National Parent-Teacher Association is holding regional forums to encourage the public to voice indignation over TV violence. The American Medical Association has asked ten major corporations to review their policies on sponsoring excessively violent shows. At least eight percent of the parent-consumers who watch TV have stopped buying products advertised on violent shows. And the movement is growing. In response, the TV networks report that the number of violent incidents on TV has declined by as much as 24 percent since 1975.[3]

However, as a concerned parent, you do not have to wait until the pressure mounts and TV violence is finally curtailed. There are things you can do now to protect your children from the harmful effects of viewing TV violence. Below are some suggestions.

Talk with your children about TV violence and the harmful effects it can have on them. Also, talk with them about what shows you consider to be excessively violent. I find that many times children agree, in which case the matter gets settled very quickly. If your younger children do not seem to understand or will not go along, you may decide that, in their best interests, excessively violent shows will be off-limits. This is what we did when our children were pre-school age. For example, as our son became old enough to enjoy TV cartoon shows, we noticed a definite increase in his aggressive behavior. At one point, he used a yardstick to hack the leaves off a favorite houseplant. When asked why he did it, he replied that he was "playing jungle." In fact, he was mimicking a TV cartoon "hero" whom he had seen hacking through the jungle in search of "the bad guys." At another point, our son began doing karate chops on his sister and neighborhood friends. Again, the aggressive behavior was a direct result of a TV cartoon show, where the "hero" used karate to subdue his opponents. After discussing the problem with our son, it became clear that he would not give up watching these violent TV cartoons voluntarily. However, we felt so strongly about the harmful effects of these shows that we were firm: there would be no more violent cartoons. For several days, our son protested; then, he realized that we meant what we said and dropped the whole thing. Our house was much more peaceful from then on.

When children get beyond pre-school age, you may

find that the imposition of limits creates battles. If so, try holding a family meeting in which the whole subject is fully discussed, and an attempt is made to come to a consensus on which shows are excessively violent. If you find it difficult or next to impossible to get a consensus, then try using the following chart (see Figure 1,). Each time force is used in a program, your children are to indicate the kind of force used by writing a very brief description of the incident and type of violence used in the appropriate space on the chart. At the end of the program, sit down with your children and discuss their findings. You may want to keep a chart yourself, so that you can compare notes. Ask the children to consider two questions about each of the violent incidents recorded: "Was the use of force in this situation justified?" and, "What other ways, if any, could the situation have been handled with less use of force?" At the very least, your children should develop an awareness of how needlessly violent many programs are.

Figure 1.

Name of program _____ Date_____

Description of the violent incident:	Was the use of violence justified?	What alternative ways could have been used to handle the situation with less violence?
1. _____	_____	_____
_____	_____	_____
2. _____	_____	_____
_____	_____	_____
etc. _____	_____	_____

Another way to help your children develop an awareness of violence on TV is to ask them to keep a log of all the TV programs they watch for one week, and to record the total number of violent incidents that occur in each program. (By the way, many of the cartoon shows on Saturday morning have the highest number of violent incidents.) Then, at the end of the week, hold a family meeting to discuss their findings.

Ask them if the real world, in their own experience, is as violent as the TV world they have just logged. Then, ask them to describe their ideal world—that is, the kind of world they would ideally like to live in. Would it have violence? Finally, ask them what effect they think the violent shows on TV have on our society. Do they help or hinder the creation of an ideal, non-violent world? If their answer is that it hinders, confirm their views by presenting the research findings on the effects of TV violence on children. (See *Remote Control*, 1978.) If their answer is that it helps, which is unlikely, challenge their views, also by presenting the research findings on TV violence. If they still remain unconvinced that violent shows should bite the dust, then be prepared to turn off the set and face the consequences.

Footnotes

[1]This information is from an article by Harry F. Walters in *Newsweek*, February 21, 1977, entitled, "What TV Does To Kids."
[2]Ibid.
[3]Ibid.

4 HOW TO DEAL WITH KIDVID COMMERCIALS

HOW TO DEAL WITH KIDVID COMMERCIALS

According to a *Newsweek* report, advertisers spent more than $400 million for the commercials on children's morning and weekend programs last year.[1] Most of this enormous outlay was designed to convince kids that they must absolutely have products of highly questionable value—sugary glop with little or no nutritional value, and toys that fall apart the first time the child gives them a real workout. Once the kids get these "message-musts" implanted in their brains, they begin to work on their parents. The merciless onslaught of a child who is totally convinced that he or she must have Fruit Flop gum or Super Sugar Krinkles to be happy is hard to resist.

Reform is coming, but so far it is coming very slowly. And children's programming may never be rid of questionable advertising. But, as with TV violence, you need not sit helplessly by and allow your children to be huckstered. There *are* things you can do:

1. Don't let your younger children watch TV programs unless the sponsors advertise worthwhile products, and do so without using misleading advertising techniques (see pages 40-43).

Then, write the TV network, local station, or sponsor and tell them what you've done and why.

2. Help your children learn to discriminate between worthwhile products and those of dubious value.

For instance, when my son was just turning four, he began begging for every toy he saw advertised on TV. Finally, at my wits end, I took him to his room and together we examined the toys he owned. The only toys that were in good working order, even after several years of hard use, were the toys made by Fisher-Price, Playskool, and Creative Playthings. Almost every other toy, especially those made by the companies that advertise the most on TV, had fallen apart or broken within the first six months of use. Apparently, my point was well made, because the begging stopped, and my son actually took pride in pointing out to anyone watching TV with him, that this or that toy wasn't any good because it was made by such and such company and therefore it would fall apart.

3. Give your children a weekly allowance.

Then, when they begin clamoring for something advertised on TV, simply tell them to save their allowance and buy it themselves. We presently give each of our children 50 cents per week. They are entitled to blow all the money on candy or ice cream during the week, if they choose, or they can save their half-dollars for several weeks, until they are able to buy a toy. Both our five- and seven-year olds are learning some valuable lessons about spending money, but best of all, they have completely stopped clamoring for things they see on TV.

4. Don't get caught at Christmas or birthdays with no choice but to buy "it."

I remember my daughter, on her sixth birthday, wanted a country store set, which she had seen advertised on TV. That's all she talked about for two months before her birthday. My wife and I didn't say no, or try to steer her in another direction, mostly because the way the set was advertised on TV was appealing, and also, it fit our back-to-the-country mood at the time. Our mistake was in not checking out the set ahead of time. When we went to buy it several days before our daughter's birthday, we found that what was in the set—a six-inch doll, a cardboard store, and an assortment of tiny plastic equipment, most of which had to be put together—was way over-priced. We were outraged. But we felt trapped. Our daughter had told all her friends that she was getting the store for her birthday, and would obviously be severely disappointed if she didn't get it.

We vowed never to be caught off-guard again. Now, we investigate ahead of time, and give our children plenty of clues that we don't think a product is worth the money, and that therefore, they are not likely to see it under the Christmas tree or in a box wrapped with birthday paper.

5. Help your child learn to recognize TV advertising propaganda for what it is.

If you are not aware of the misleading techniques

used by many advertisers to induce people to buy their products, then learn to recognize the major offenders. Read your children the descriptions below, and then, during a TV ad, ask them to see if they can recognize any of the techniques being used. They will learn to identify the fallacies of such ads in short order, and will no longer be quite so naive and vulnerable to specious advertising claims.

ADVERTISING TECHNIQUES

A. *Testimonials* In this type of ad, a distinguished person, or for that matter, just a plain citizen, gives• a testimonial recommending the use of the product. What one must remember is, that just because a distinguished person, such as a famous athlete for example, recommends the product, that does not mean that he or she uses it regularly, or that it is a good product or the best brand available. Remember, the person giving the testimonial is being paid to do so, and this can influence him or her to recommend a product which that person might not otherwise recommend. Here is an example of a testimonial ad: "Hi. I'm Johnny King (a famous athlete). I eat Super Sugar Plops every day! How about you? Have Mom get some today and try them. You'll love Super Sugar Plops as much as I do!"

B. *Prestige by Association* In this type of ad, the sellers display their product along with an object of high prestige, in the hope that some of the prestige of the object will rub off on their product. What we must remember is, that just because the product is shown or associated with something that we value, that does not mean that the product is therefore of more value than it would be otherwise, or that what happens in the ad will happen that way for us. Example: A bicycle manufacturer introduces a new high-priced model by showing a boy sitting on the bike surrounded by a group of admiring adolescents. (Hidden message: "Buy this bike and you will be the center of attention and have lots of admiring friends.")

C. *Repetition* In this type of commercial, a slogan or jingle is repeated a number of times. Also, the same commercial is likely to be repeated several times in the same program. The object of the ad is to keep the slogan or jingle in front of the viewer until the words become implanted in his/her mind. To attest to the effectiveness of this ploy, how often do you catch yourself or your children singing a jingle like the Coca-Cola song, "I'd love to teach the world to sing. . . ." What we must remember is, that just because a slogan or jingle is repeated again and again, that does not necessarily make it true or desirable.

D. *Emotional Appeal* In this type of ad, emotion-ally-loaded words and pictures are used to make the product look more appealing than it actually is. For example, an army doll is shown being played with by two boys on a rugged mountain terrain. Also, many accessory items are pictured, which must be purchased separately. What we must remember is, such TV ads may indeed arouse our interest or fantasy, but that does not mean that the product will be able to deliver what we want from it.

Footnote

[1]Harry F. Walters, "What TV Does To Kids," *Newsweek*, February 21, 1977.

5 HOW TO HELP YOUR CHILD KICK THE TV HABIT

HOW TO HELP YOUR CHILD
KICK THE TV HABIT

In her book, *The Plug-In Drug,* Marie Winn writes that, "not unlike drugs or alcohol, the television experience allows the participant to blot out the real world and enter into a pleasurable and passive mental state [where] the worries and anxieties of reality are as effectively deferred by becoming absorbed in a television program as by going on a "trip" induced by drugs or alcohol."[1] Ms. Winn goes on to make a very convincing case that television can become so habit-forming and addictive for many adults and children, that it simply controls much of their lives. Ms. Winn believes that this is especially disturbing in the case of children, because children who are addicted to TV simply do not engage in socially and intellectually stimulating activities.

If, as a parent, you have any indication that your child is becoming hooked on TV, you might well consider the problem to be just as serious as if your child were becoming hooked on drugs or alcohol. Perhaps the physical consequences of TV addiction are not as serious as the physical consequences of alcohol or drug addiction, but the psychological, social, and intellectual damage that TV can produce may be just as severe.[2] Here is a checklist of behaviors that you might want to

consider:
  If your child:
  —insists on watching TV rather than playing or do-
    ing other things;
  —views TV as if he or she is in a stupor;
  —tries to strike desperate bargains ("If you let me
    watch ten more minutes, I won't watch at all
    tomorrow.");
  —will watch anything anytime rather than turn off
    the set;
  —would rather watch a completely blurred image
    rather than turn it off;
then you may have a TV addict on your hands. Helping your child kick the TV habit won't be easy, but it
is not impossible. Here are some suggestions:

**1. If your children are between the ages of one
month to six years, turn the TV set off, except,
perhaps, for special occasions.**

Then, get your children involved in creative play
both individually and with other children. At this stage
of the game, your children can become unhooked as
easily as they became hooked. But remember, if you
are conscientious in interesting them in other activities
early on, your children need never get hooked on TV in
the first place.

**2. Don't expect your children to kick the TV habit
alone.**

Help them to make the transition by spending time
getting them started on alternative activities and taking

a genuine interest in what they are doing. A lack of interest and attention on your part can drive them right back to the tube.

3. Help your children, especially older children, think of alternatives to watching TV.

For example, have your children make a list of all the things they really like to do. The list should include games they like to play, crafts, hobbies, projects, places to visit, and so on—as well as watching TV. Then, help each child estimate how much time he or she spends on each activity. If TV comes out higher than the others, ask your children if they can think of better ways to spend their time. Explain that television programs may give them valuable information, but games and other play activities help to develop their imaginations, social skills, and creative abilities. Help them plan to do more of the things they like to do, other than watching TV. Post the lists so that they can be consulted whenever your children become bored and are inclined to turn on the TV.

4. Another approach to developing alternatives to TV is to sit down as a family, and make a list of all the new things that your children have never done but might try to do instead of watching TV.

Put all the ideas on the list without discussing or evaluating them. Even unfeasible ideas may help to trigger ideas that really might be useful. Later, family members can go back and cross out items that might be too dangerous, dull, or impractical. Then, help your children make plans to try some of the activities instead of watching TV. Post the list for easy reference.

5. As children move closer to living their ideal day, they become more satisfied and energetic, and thus less dependent upon TV as a means of relieving the boredom and frustration which comes from living a ho-hum, humdrum existence.

To help your children move closer to living their ideal day, have them make a list of the things that they actually do during an average day. (The focus can be on a day during the week or weekend, vacation or school year.) Include things like sleeping, eating, playing, watching TV, reading, doing homework, etc. Then, they are to estimate the average number of hours or minutes they spend on each activity during the day. Now, have your children think about what an ideal day would look like for them. Have them make a list of the things they would like to do if they were completely free to choose, and then allocate the average number of hours or minutes they would like to spend doing each activity. Finally, help your children to examine possible ways they could move closer to living their ideal day. This might require some negotiation, problem-solving, and/or conflict resolution.

6. One of the reasons that children often watch a lot of TV is that they lack any clear direction or purpose in their lives.

TV simply becomes a way of killing time, and thus not feeling the boredom of drifting through life. If your children fit into this category, you may be able to help them stop drifting by getting them to identify some of the goals that they think are worth achieving.

The following two activities can be used to help your children identify some worthwhile goals and get started on them. The first activity can be used with children of all ages; the second activity is a much more in-depth treatment, and is designed for older children and teenagers.

Activity #1: For Use With Any Age Child

Have your child use or make a chart like the one below (see Figure 2). In the first column, have him/her list for each item, something he/she would like to learn to do or be able to do better. In the second column, he/she is to list for each item a first step he/she could take to get started. Then, have your child decide which things he/she really wants to do, and what would be a realistic timetable for doing them. Enter the date he/she plans to get started in the third column.

Activity #2: For Use With Older Children

This activity can be used to help your older child or teenager develop a plan of action to give his or her life direction.

Have your child make a list of goals by posing the following questions:

A. What are your educational goals? (Sample responses: "I want to get better grades." "I want to go to college.")

B. What are your family goals? (Sample responses: "I want to get along better with my sister." "I want to take more family trips.")

Figure 2.		
What I'd Like To Do or Be Able To Do Better.	A First Step I Can Take.	Date To Get Started

C. What are your friendship or social goals? (Sample responses: "I want to have more friends." "I want to have more influence with my friends.")

D. What are your leisure-time goals? (Sample responses: "I want to learn to play the guitar." "I want to spend my free time more productively.")

E. What are your personal growth goals? (Sample responses: "I want to lose weight." "I want to be more spontaneous and worry less.")

F. What are your vocational or career goals? (Sample responses: "I want to explore several alternatives by getting a summer job in each of these fields." "I want to get a good-paying part-time job after school.")

G. What are your long range-life goals? (Sample responses: "I want to make an important contribution." "I want to have a simple lifestyle that is close to the earth.")

H. What other goals do you have?

Then, for each of the above goals, help your child to answer the following questions:

A. What obstacle could keep you from reaching this goal if you take this action? (This might include such obstacles as fear of failure, lack of self-confidence, lack of skills, others who might try to block you.)

B. What are some things you could do or steps you could take to make sure these obstacles don't block you?

C. Whom could you get to help you? What kind of help could each person give?

D. What are your chances for success? What makes you think this?

E. What are some good things that might happen if you succeeded? Failed?

F. What are some negative things that might happen if you succeeded? Failed?

7. Here's a strategy that helps children look at TV viewing in a new light.

Have each family member complete the following sentence stems:

The high point for me this weekend was _____.

The high point for me this week was _____.

The high point for me this month was _____.

The high point for me this year was _____.

Hold a family meeting in which each person gets to share his/her high points. Then, ask each person to note how many of their high points were watching TV. In our experience, very few people put TV viewing as a high point. Then, ask each person to estimate how much time they spend watching TV versus doing the things which they put down as high points. Finally, help each family member or the family as a whole make plans to do more of the things that they really enjoy doing.

Inadvertently, our family discovered this strategy on a two-week vacation in the mountains where TV was not available. One evening, our seven-year-old daughter asked why we didn't have this much fun back home. One of our conclusions was that the TV set kept us from doing fun things as a family. Our daughter then suggested that we should put the TV away for awhile, which we did. This action has made a real difference in our lives. We now do many more things as a family, like playing games, doing projects, and taking trips. We still watch TV occasionally, but only when something really worth viewing comes on.

8. Locate the TV set in an out-of-the-way place in the house.

For example, we keep our TV set in the master bedroom closet when it is not being used. Thus, our children must come and ask us to get the set out of the closet and move it into the hall or downstairs when they want to watch a program. Right away, this procedure cuts out the possibility that the kids can just flip on the set whenever they want. It also gives us control over the set, since we can ask questions, like what they want to watch and whether it is worth watching, as well as how many hours they have watched TV that week. Furthermore, it becomes a bit of a hassle for the kids to watch TV, and thus they often decide that it isn't worth the effort. The basement or attic are also good storage areas for the TV, since the set is then less accessible—"out of sight, out of mind."

Footnotes

[1]Winn, Marie, *The Plug-In Drug: Television, Children and the Family*, The Viking Press, New York, 1977.
[2]For more on this, see Marie Winn's *The Plug-In Drug*.

6 HOW TO DEAL WITH YOUR CHILD'S TV-RELATED EMOTIONAL UPSETS

HOW TO DEAL WITH YOUR CHILD'S TV-RELATED EMOTIONAL UPSETS

Television can have a powerful emotional effect upon our children. For example, one evening my daughter was watching *Lassie*. In this particular episode, Lassie got trapped in a cave. My daughter, who was four at the time, started crying and shaking. She was very afraid that the dog would be hurt. I can also recall other times when television programs have had similar effects upon my own and other children. The question is, how should we handle our child's TV-related emotional upsets? To answer this question, I shall use the following illustration.

Let's say that a mother and her young son are shopping in a large and crowded department store. Somehow the mother and child get separated for about five minutes. The mother is frantic. The child becomes very frightened and emotionally upset. Upon being reunited with her son, the mother might do one of the following:

1. She might admonish or punish the child for straying away.

2. She might feel guilty about letting her son get out of her sight, and thus load the child with sympathy.
3. She might feel embarrassed by her son's natural display of emotion over being lost, and thus try to silence his crying.
4. She might feel anger at the child and/or herself, and thus simply ignore his emotional state by going on about her shopping.
5. She might take her son in her arms and give him her full, warm attention until his crying subsides.

If the mother does any of steps 1 through 4, she practically guarantees that her son will spend the rest of the shopping trip emotionally upset and clutching her skirt to make sure he doesn't get separated again, and that the next time they are in a similar situation, he will act much the same by becoming emotionally upset, anxious, frightened, and irrational. However, if she does step 5, the child will most likely spend considerable time crying, trembling, and perhaps being angry with her for losing him, but once he has got all the emotions out of his system, he will probably spend the rest of the shopping trip in normal spirits. He will also learn a valuable lesson, that in crowded situations it is best to keep an eye on the person he is with, and stay near that person.

How can we account for this difference? Perhaps our emotions serve a very real purpose in the human body. When children get hurt, either physically or psychologically, their natural response is to cry. (Being lost or rejected can be just as damaging psychologically as getting banged on the head, skinning a knee, or cutting a finger is physically damaging.) In a very real sense, human emotions are apparently a part of the body's natural healing process for psychological distress. When children are allowed to express their *grief* or *sorrow* through tears, *fear* through trembling and shaking, and *anger* through storming, they are then able to deal with the distressing situation in a much more rational and effective way. However, when they are prevented from expressing these emotions, the grief, fear, and anger remain all balled up inside them, and any situation which reminds them in some way of the original distressing experience will trigger a renewal of the unpleasant emotions.[1]

The difficulty is, that in our culture, neither children nor adults are encouraged to recognize and express their emotions in hurtful or distressing situations. For example, how many times have you heard these phrases addressed to children?

—Don't be such a cry-baby!

—Don't be such a scaredy-cat!

—Stop that crying, or I'll *really* give you something to cry about!

—Big boys don't cry.

—I want you to act like a lady instead of like a spoiled brat.

The fact is, that we actively discourage children

and adults from displaying their emotions except in the most traumatic situations, and even then, we will, more likely than not, actively try to quiet them by patting and stroking them and repeating a phrase like, "Don't take it so hard, honey," or by trying to make light of the situation: "It's really nothing, dear." Perhaps we equate the tears with being sorrowful, and the trembling with being afraid, and since we don't want our children to go through life being sorrowful or afraid, we prevent them from expressing these emotions. Ironically, by doing so, we may well insure that the distressing experience remains locked up inside our children. Or, perhaps the crying, shaking, and storming of our children triggers old fears, griefs, and angers within us, and thus we have to subdue our children for fear we will also find ourselves trembling, crying, or losing our tempers. Whatever the case, psychologists tell us that we are doing a great deal of emotional damage to our children by preventing or discouraging them from expressing their emotions and feelings.[2] The problem is particularly acute for little boys, from whom we demand an even greater emotional stoicism than from little girls.

To get back to the situation with my daughter and the TV program *Lassie,* apparently the dog's being lost triggered some fear that my daughter had not fully resolved. As I searched her past, I eventually recalled that when she was about two, she had got separated from the family at a very large and crowded farmer's market. She was only lost for a few minutes, but the experience frightened her considerably. I remembered that she cried for quite some time, and that we had to carry her for the rest of the trip. Undoubtedly, we were in a hurry to resume our shopping and thus didn't take the time that our daughter needed to fully resolve her fears. As a result, perhaps there was enough similarity between Lassie being lost and our daughter's being lost herself to bring on her emotional upset.

WHAT TO DO ABOUT IT

When faced with a child who has become emotionally upset, child psychologists tell us to:

1. Give the emotionally upset child your full, undivided attention.
Hold the child. Put your arms around the child. Tell the child that it is OK to be afraid and to cry. Don't pat or stroke the child, as this may be interpreted as an attempt to curb an emotional display. Don't provide sympathy, as this, too, seems to shut off feelings. Just give the child your attention and encourage the child to express thoughts and feelings. The child will do the rest.

2. If the child is upset but goes to his or her room and shuts the door to keep you out, ask the child if you can talk with him or her for a few minutes.
If the child agrees, try to help him or her understand what is going on. For example, you might say, "Sometimes, TV shows or other things make us feel bad. They make us feel like crying, or getting angry, or being afraid. If we keep those feelings inside, we con-

tinue to feel bad. When we are feeling bad about ourselves, we often do very hurtful things to ourselves and to others. But if we let those bad feelings out, they go away almost like magic, and suddenly we feel better."

Tell the child that you want to listen to his or her bad feelings and help resolve them. If the child still resists, try to find out what is causing the resistance. Perhaps the child believes that you really don't care. For example, you may have discouraged the child from expressing feelings in the past. If this is the case, tell the child that you were wrong not to have listened before, and that you want to correct that mistake. If you really mean it, it won't take long for the child to respond.

3. Sometimes, you can help the child talk about the experiences that caused the feelings of distress in the first place.

Questions like, "Have you ever felt this way before?" can help the child recall earlier experiences. With the recall will often come the feelings and thoughts that the child felt at the time but never resolved. Encourage the child to tell you about those feelings or thoughts. Once the old distress experience is fully resolved, it won't be there to get triggered in the future.

For information on handling emotionally-upset children, see Thomas Gordon's, *Parent Effectiveness Training*, Wyden, New York, 1973.

Footnotes

[1]Jackins, Harvey, *The Human Side of Human Beings*, Rational Island Press, Seattle, Washington, 1964.
[2]Rogers, Carl R., *On Becoming A Person*, Houghton Mifflin, Boston, 1961, and Gordon, Thomas, *Parent Effectiveness Training*, Wyden, New York, 1973.

HOW TO INFLUENCE TELEVISION PROGRAMMING

HOW TO INFLUENCE
TELEVISION PROGRAMMING

Never underestimate the power of individual action. Television executives are quite aware of the ratings, and they realize that ratings are determined by a representative sample of viewers. In other words, ratings are established by analyzing the responses of a small number of viewers, and then enlarging that number in a statistical format. The number of complaints that a television station receives is often an indication of viewer rejection or acceptance of certain programs or actions. When there is an unusual amount of correspondence, either by letter or by telephone, the station pays close attention to the trend of the correspondence.

When an individual communicates with a TV station, the result is that management becomes *aware* of the viewer's feelings. Although one phone call may not result in the cancellation of a television game show or series, the complaint does have an effect. Making the proper person aware of a particular complaint is very important. Awareness is important in the selection of future programming. For instance, when management considers choosing a new program or airing additional programs, phone calls, favorable or negative, might make the difference in the choice between two shows.

Suggestions may spark ideas in a program director's decision-making process.

Therefore, if you feel strongly, either for or against a program or series, write a letter or pick up the telephone and tell the station how you feel. If you call, tell the station's receptionist that you want to speak with the programming director. Writing a letter is even better. It shows that you were interested enough to spend time to put your thoughts on paper. Also, a letter contains concrete statements and can not be forgotten or misrepresented. A letter speaks for itself. If it is possible, a letter or other communication should be specific in what the viewer found good or bad in the TV show. Arguments about taste do not change the ratings. If a show has good ratings, the network will not care if some viewers consider the program to be in bad taste. If, however, a show *is* in poor taste, it is important to describe what is in poor taste. The whole question of taste is subjective, and in communicating with television management, try to be specific. To be most effective, your communication should contain as much information as possible, as if you were making the programming choice yourself.

Many stations employ a person called an executive producer. The executive producer oversees the production of programs at the station, and would be responsive to suggestions made by the station. Perhaps there are some points in a program produced at the station which could be improved or eliminated in future productions. In that case, a communication with the executive producer might be in order.

At the end of a program watch for the names of the persons who are associated with the program. The listing of activities and the persons who performed those activities are referred to as the credits, and are generally shown at the end of the program. The executive producer is the person who is the top decision-maker for the program or series. The producer carries out the production. If you have a particular comment with respect to one of the activities in the production, you might wish to communicate directly with one of the persons listed.

In communicating with particular individuals, make sure that you notice *where* the program was produced. The last credit identifies the production company. The production company may be located at the local station, but generally it is located elsewhere.

The vast majority of programs are network programs. Network programs are generally made at the large studios, such as Universal, Warner Brothers, Tandem Productions, and so on, and then are sold to or carried by the networks. Sometimes, the networks will produce their own programs, as well as buying programs produced at the large studios.

The three commercial networks (ABC, CBS, and NBC) present the bulk of the programming with national distribution and therefore have the most important role in the choice of programming. Local stations carry most of the network programs. Occasionally, a local station will choose to broadcast a program other than the network program, but generally the network shows will be carried. If you want to go directly to the source, write to the network executives:

ABC
Vice President For Programming
1330 Avenue of the Americas
New York, New York 10019
212 - LT1-7777

CBS
Vice President For Programming
51 W. 52nd Street
New York, New York 10019
212-765-4321

NBC
30 Rockefeller Plaza
New York, New York 10020
212-Circle 7-8300

Corporation For Public Broadcasting
888 16th Street, N.W.
Washington, D.C. 20006
202-293-6260

For Public Television, it is best to communicate with the local station, as each local station does exercise a very active role in its own programming of these shows.

UHF stations, for the most part, carry reruns of old shows and sporting events. Often, children will watch UHF channels after school. The reason for this is that many afternoon programs are talk shows aimed at adult audiences. Therefore, children will tune in the UHF stations, which carry reruns of children's shows.

A tremendous number of commercials often seem to interrupt the UHF reruns during the hours when children are watching UHF broadcasts. It might be worthwhile to monitor the number of minutes devoted to commercials during reruns, as there is a limit placed on commercial time by FCC regulations. You might wish to compare the number of commercials carried on UHF stations with the amount of commercial time spent by the VHF stations.

If there appears to be an unreasonable number of commercials on UHF stations in comparison with VHF (2-13) stations, you may wish to write to or call the Federal Communications Commission:

The Federal Communications Commission
1919 M. Street, N.W.
Washington, D.C. 20036
202-655-4000

Office of Reports and Information—Room 202
Office of the Executive Director—Room 352
Complaints and Compliance Division—Room A304
Public Records Room—Room 239

For information about television, you should contact:

The Television Information Office (The Library)
747 Fifth Ave.
New York, New York 10022
212-PL9-6800

The Television Information Office has a marvelous library of television information.

One of the most dynamic and active groups dedicated to the improvement of children's television is:

Action For Children's Television (ACT)
46 Austin Street
Newtonville, Mass. 02160
617-527-7870

ACT aims "to educate and enlighten parents and others involved with children to the importance of television's effects on the child;

"To pressure and persuade broadcasters and advertisers to provide programming of the highest quality designed for children of different ages;

"To eliminate commercialism from children's programs and to substitute a new system of financial support, including underwriting and public service funding."

ACT invites parents to send for free information, and offers a membership opportunity for anyone who wishes to join this group. There is a very modest membership fee.

Participation in ACT is encouraged, as ACT represents an important bloc of parents lobbying for children. ACT consists mainly of parents, who do quite an effective job of focusing attention on what is good and what is bad on TV.

If you are really disturbed about something on television, and feel that a special protest must be made, send a letter to your senator or congressman with copies of your correspondence with the networks. Generally, the senator will ask one of his staff members to look into your statement, and he might follow it up with an inquiry on your behalf.

Television stations are licensed regularly by the government, and must have their licenses reviewed in order to continue operating. One of the greatest threats to the station is a challenge to their licenses. Disenchanted and dissatisfied citizens can prompt the government to take a very close look at a particular TV station. Therefore, by speaking out, you can exercise a tremendous force in seeing that stations operate properly.

If your complaint is justified, rest assured that others feel the same way. Your letter might not be the only one on the subject, and a number of letters voicing the same complaint might have a significant impact on the actions of a station or of a network. Therefore, do not hesitate to act! Your letter might make a crucial difference in what is shown on television.

*By Bernard Solomon

PART II

HOW TO MAKE TELEVISION A POSITIVE EXPERIENCE FOR YOUR CHILD

8 INTRODUCTION TO PART II

INTRODUCTION TO PART II

Consider the following:

- Among children who watch *Sesame Street* on a regular basis, those who gain most have mothers or fathers who often watch the show with them and talk with them about it.[1]

- Prime Time School Television, a nonprofit Chicago organization, uses some of television's most violent programs to teach positive social values to children and adolescents. Adult intervention is the key to the project's success.[2]

- The Philadelphia Schools' TV Reading Project has pupils watch popular television programs while following along in network scripts. Teacher-led discussions and creative re-enactments of the shows are then done in class. The project is so successful— some pupils' reading skills have advanced by three years—that 3,500 other U.S. school systems are adopting the plan.[3]

- In a February, 1977 issue of *Newsweek*, entitled "What TV Does To Kids," the author concludes that, "Virtually all experts agree on one palliative for parents of all socioeconomic levels. Instead of using TV as an electronic baby-sitter, parents must try to involve themselves directly in their youngsters' viewing. By watching along with the kids at least occasionally, they can help them evaluate what they see—pointing out the inflated claims of a commercial, perhaps, or criticizing a gratuitously violent scene."

This part of the book is designed to help you make television a positive experience for your child by directly involving yourself in his or her viewing. We have included chapters on how to use television to nurture your child's learning power and value development; how to answer your child's TV questions; how to use TV in the classroom; and how to use TV as a creative babysitter.

Footnotes

[1]Lesser, Gerald, S., *Children and Television,* Vintage, New York, 1974.
[2]Walters, Harry F., "What TV Does To Kids," *Newsweek,* February 21, 1977.
[3]Mankiewicz, Frank and Joel Swerdlow, *Remote Control,* Times Books, New York, 1978.

9 HOW TO USE TV TO INCREASE YOUR CHILD'S LEARNING POWER

THE SKILL OF IDENTIFYING THE MAIN IDEA AND SUPPORTING DETAILS

Children are frequently tested in school on their ability to identify the main idea of a story. Frequently, children are placed on a lower reading level because they have made errors in identifying the main ideas. Sometimes, they may refer to a supporting detail, to a point of interest, or to an isolated fact. Unfortunately, children will refer to points of interest and might not understand what is meant by the main idea. Therefore, if the common identifiable theme can be brought out, you are doing your children an enormous favor by directing their thinking.

Activities:

1. Take the TV section from the daily newspaper or TV Guide, and cut out the short "story summaries" about each show that your child is about to watch (or watched the previous night).

Cut each show out without the name of the program (or draw a line through the name so that the child can not see the title). Mix up the pieces and ask your child to match the names of the shows with the stories.

2. Ask your child to write a statement that would entice a viewer to tune in to a program.

Limit your child to 10 or fifteen words. The child then becomes a writer for the newspaper. The child's statement should be similar to what appears in the daily television column. Generally, there is only enough space for a sentence, and often these sentences tell nothing. However, writing program-summaries is an excellent activity. George Bernard Shaw once wrote, "I sent you a long letter because I did not have time to write you a short one." Clarity and brevity are virtues, and this activity helps children to express themselves concisely.

3. Have your child read, or read to your child, the column in the newspaper telling about the program about to be seen.

Usually, there is a local newspaper writer who has previewed the program; this writer devotes part of his or her daily column to a critique of the program. Sometimes, the column is devoted to a review of the program shown the night before. In the same format used in your local paper, ask your child to write a similar column. If you feel that this might be too difficult, ask your child to tell you how he or she would have you write the column. You may wish to actually write a column based on what your child told you, and then ask the child to read the column aloud. He or she might make corrections, or let the column stand; in either event, the child has participated in a learning experience.

4. Ask your child to think of an appropriate title for an episode that he or she has just watched.

Many programs have titles for each episode. For example: *Sanford and Son:* "Mama's Baby, Papa's Maybe." Have your child think of an alternative title. This is a good opportunity to develop your child's thinking and summarizing skills.

5. Who is the hero or heroine of the program?

Generally, on a weekly series, this person is identified as the star of the series. But on some programs and movies, it might take some time to see who is the hero. Therefore, at the beginning, middle, and end of the show, it might be helpful to ask your child who the good guys and the bad guys are. You might also ask who is the hero or star.

6. An important question to ask and discuss is whether the program is true or false to reality.

Many times young children will become frightened with what they see on television. You might not even know that they are frightened, but you may learn this in the middle of the night, if the child has a nightmare. Therefore, with some shows that have a high degree of adventure or suspense, (and certainly with cartoons peopled by monsters, and such), you might want to ask the child if the situation or characters are realistic. You might be surprised to find out how often your child thinks that what he or she is watching is real. Many times a parent will assume something. With television—don't assume. Ask!

7. Documentaries give information.

News presents short headlines of happenings. However, documentaries often have a point of view. Determining the difference between fact and opinion is a skill tested in basic standardized tests, and is important in reading and language arts. It certainly is important for adults to know the difference between fact and opinion. Therefore, try to choose a story that is also a documentary. A story about another country or a special event usually is a good working possibility. Also, some of the animal programs are excellent documentaries, as they have a narration which often offers some comment to heighten the interest level. After a statement has been made which is obviously a matter of opinion, ask your child to identify the statement as fact or opinion. This is a good beginning. Use the same exercise when a factual statement is made. If you can point out a subtle opinion, do so. Once you have brought out the concept of fact and opinion, you might wish to move on to the news. Here, although it may be very subtle, opinion is often infused into the facts. You might wish to go to the library and read up on propaganda techniques for this exercise. During the news, comment is supposed to be titled "comment," either by a statement to that effect or by the word "comment" appearing on the screen.

8. There are many types of programs: situation comedies, adventure stories, mysteries, suspense

stories, dramas, variety shows, news, documentaries, soap operas, sports, cartoons, and so on.

To increase your child's awareness of these categories, ask him or her what type of program is being shown. After discussing film categories, you might encourage your child to apply these classifications to books—and perhaps follow up the discussion with a trip to the library.

* 9.   Turn off the volume, leaving on the picture.

Ask your child to tell you what is happening.

10.   Leave the volume on.

Ask your child to close his eyes and describe the visual scene.

11.   When the commercials come on, follow the procedure outlined above, by turning off the volume and listening to what your child says is happening.

Also, by having your child close his or her eyes and listen, he or she will try to describe what he or she envisions. Sometimes, your child will have already seen the commercial. In that case, don't abandon the exercise. The skill of recall is an important skill in learning to read.

12.   During a commercial, ask your child to tell you what is going to happen.

This exercise uses the skill of prediction, another basic skill in reading and language arts. This is also a good technique on crime shows and on situation comedies. Comedies are unpredictable, but predicting the unpredictable presents an exciting challenge.

13. Ask your child to explain why a particular show might be considered a "hit."

14. After a television show, ask your child to draw a picture which portrays the "feeling" of the show.
Discuss the picture with your child, asking why he or she portrayed certain feelings, or why he or she chose to draw certain things. Ask why the child chose those things and not other things. Ask if the child felt that the choice had any personal significance. The child may wish to relate some personal feeling, and there is a good chance that a family discussion on an important topic will evolve. If it does not, you have still developed your child's organizational skills and critical thinking.

15. Ask your child to draw a cartoon with three to ten squares (depending on the age of the child).
Then ask your child to depict the story development in these squares. Here you are helping your child to distinguish between main ideas and supporting details, to analyze the plot, and to actually outline the program. This is an exercise in summary, plot, and imagination, as the cartoon drawings are representations of creativity.

USING TELEVISION TO GENERATE INTEREST IN READING

How often can you remember a teacher taking away a comic book from a student? Without a doubt, a child should be paying attention to the teacher rather than looking at a comic book. Even if teachers cannot be expected to offer stimulating, attention-getting performances all the time, children should still have the self-discipline and respect for authority not to resort to entertainment material during class—or so the argument goes.

Perhaps, on the other hand, educators should take advantage of anything that, through the child's interest, can become an exercise in reading. If the child is reading comic books, then use the comic books to develop reading skills.

This admonition also applies to parents. Why not take advantage of what interests your child? If television is the prime source of your child's entertainment, then capitalize on that interest. If your child wants a comic book based on a television series or cartoon, buy the comic book. But buy only one comic book and make conditions; the child can't buy another comic book until he has read the first one.

Often, a child will not read a comic, but will merely look at the pictures. Also, many comics have a lengthy narrative, which is not included in the bubbles encompassing the characters' dialogue. The vocabulary of the narrative is often rather sophisticated, and the concepts may even be quite complicated. Therefore, if your child has an interest in the comic's story-line, you should do all you can to encourage and help him read the narrative portions of the comic book.

1. Let your child read the comic book.
When he or she has finished reading, ask if you can

borrow the comic book for a while. Then, ask the child some questions:

A. How many stories were in the comic book?
B. What was the plot, or plots?
C. Who were the main characters?
D. Who was the hero or heroine?
E. Who were the heroes or the villains?

2. Look at the comic and choose some words from the dialogue.

Ask the child the meaning of the words (vocabulary). If the child does not know what the words mean, let the child look at the sentence (learning vocabulary from context). If the child cannot discern the meaning of the word from the context, then send the child to the dictionary to look up the word.

Do the same with the vocabulary in the narrative sections. These written statements are frequently ignored by children. Too many children just look at the pictures. But here is where you can change the procedure, and increase your child's learning power.

3. Ask your child for permission to cut out part of the comic book.

Cut out several boxes (pictures) from the different stories, and ask your child to separate the pictures into their correct and respective stories. Then, ask your child to place the boxes (pictures) from the stories in their proper sequence.

Cut out only a few pictures and ask your child to describe, by looking at the rest of the comic, what was contained in the missing boxes (context clues).

When you are satisfied that your child has learned something, then you might permit him or her to have another comic book.

Once you have developed the critical skills of reading the comics, you may then purchase or take out from the library books or paperbacks with similar stories. Your ultimate goal will be to move from comics to more mature reading material. Many television progams are based upon best-selling children's books. Examples: *Black Beauty, The Little House on the Prairie,* Nancy Drew mysteries, Hardy Boy adventures.

MATH SKILLS:

1. Ask your child to time a television program from the beginning of the hour to the conclusion of the hour (or half-hour).

The child will ultimately ask—or you will ultimately discuss—whether or not the hour (or half-hour) includes commercials. You, naturally, mean *without* commercials. You do not need a stop watch, as a clock with a second-hand is perfect. Subtraction skills will be used to get the total "show time."

2. Ask your child to time the commercials—to time the duration of individual commercials, and then to add up these sums for the total commercial time.

3. Ask your child to determine how much time in an evening (estimate total television viewing time) is spent watching commercials by multiplying the number of minutes per half-hour (or hour) by the

total number of hours of TV watched during the evening.

4. Take the television page of the newspaper and ask your child to list the shows that he or she intends to watch.

A. Ask the child how long each show lasts. (addition)

B. How long are all the shows that he is going to watch? (addition)

C. What is the average length of time for each show? (Take the total minutes and divide by the number of shows: division)

D. How many half hours are there in the viewing time? (divide by thirty: division)

E. How many hours are there in the viewing time? (divide by sixty: division)

F. How many commercial minutes are there in an evening's worth of viewing? (multiply the half-hour count by the number of half-hours—or use hours— etc.: multiplication)

G. Ask your child to calculate how many hours he spends in class with his teacher (not counting lunch and recess). Compare the number of hours spent in school each day with the number of hours spent watching television each night.

H. Ask your child to determine how many hours are spent watching television during the weekend. Add these hours to the week's viewing time and compare the total viewing time with the number of hours spent in the classroom.

I. Ask your child to determine how many hours are spent watching television during summer vacations, and holiday vacations. Add these hours to the number of viewing hours.

After using all these math skills, you and your child may eventually come to the conclusion that more time is spent watching television than watching teachers!

5. Have your child:

A. Take the television section from the Sunday paper, or buy a copy of *TV Guide.*

B. Count the number of programs (regardless of length of time) on one channel for one *weekday.*

C. Add the number of programs which appear on a different channel over the same time period.

D. Compare the number of programs on each channel over the same time period. If there is a difference, there might be more long features— such as sporting events, movies, etc. on one channel than on another. This analysis will make your child aware of the programming specialties of each station.

E. Determine the number of programs on *weekends* (compute Saturday and Sunday programs separately).

F. Compare weekend shows with weekday shows, and investigate any differences in programming. (You might want to ask why certain programs appear on certain days, why certain programs are on at certain times. This is an exercise in demographics, and will sharpen your child's scientific skills. Your child will realize that network personnel study the population's viewing habits, and that certain shows are aired for women viewers, men, children, different age groups, and so on. This strategy is particularly evident when commercial programming is studied. Notice when antacids are advertised—after dinner. Some shows which appeal to women have advertisements about products which only women would buy.

G. Determine how many shows appear all week on all channels. Do not forget to consider the UHF stations and the public broadcasting stations.

Although this series of activities basically involves math, it is also a consciousness-raising exercise. It may be possible to watch only one channel at one time, but when all the television broadcasting which is available to you is considered, the enormous scope of the TV industry becomes clear. Perhaps we, as adults and citizens, should take this electronic device more seriously. We think seriously when we spend money on a book. We spend time when we buy a magazine. How much time do we spend thinking before we watch TV?

CREATIVE WRITING SKILLS

*1. Have your child write an episode for his/her favorite television program.

*2. Have your child write a new ending to a program he/she has just viewed.

*3. Have your child rewrite an episode by adding new characters, changing the way the hero reacted at a critical point in the program, making up new events in the story, or changing the setting.

CREATIVE DRAMATICS

*1. Have your children act out their own version of a television program that they have recently viewed.

*2. Have your children put on a puppet show based upon their favorite TV characters. Simple hand-puppets can be made by drawing faces on paper lunch bags and cutting holes in the sides for "little finger and thumb arms."

SCIENCE SKILLS

*1. Encourage your child to follow up television science specials by doing a project or conducting an experiment; e.g., making a model rocket, starting a rock or insect collection, visiting a wildlife preserve.

*2. Have your child write and "produce" a short science special on a topic of his or her interest; e.g., water pollution, animals, prehistoric times.

*Thanks to Mary Martha Howe for suggesting these activities.

USING THE AUDIO CASSETTE RECORDER WITH
TELEVISION TO INCREASE SKILL DEVELOPMENT

The audio cassette, and the phenomenal decrease in the cost of cassette recorders, has brought about a great expansion in the home-entertainment electronics field. Many families own cassette recorders, and nearly everyone knows someone who will permit the borrowing of their recorder. You should not ignore using this medium to increase your child's learning power.

The audio cassette recorder can be a miniature "television" or radio broadcasting station. The cassette recorder, with its record and playback capacity and microphone, permits simulation of radio, and of the audio part of television programs. Therefore, you can do the following activities with your child on an audio cassette recorder:

1. Clip items from the newspaper which have special interest for your child. Assign your child to work a news item as an assignment editor would do. Determine how much "air time" the story deserves (allow your child to help in this decision by discussing the item's importance.)

As a follow-up to the television/radio newsroom (if you have aimed at sequence and main idea as the instructional goals), you may ask your child to "chart" the news topics and their respective air times by viewing/listening to a half-hour news program. He might be asked to list 1) the topic of the story (main idea), 2) the air time, and 3) the reason for where the story was placed in the program (sequence).

If creative writing and current events are the skills you wish to sharpen, you might ask your child to create a "feature" (a five- or ten-minute story) or even a special in-depth documentary on the desired topic (current events).

2.   Tell your child that he/she is to pretend that he/she has been employed as an advertising account executive (one who is responsible for making commercials for a particular company or organization). Your child may be the copy writer (the one who writes the commercial copy) or the announcer. As a family, choose the subject to be advertised: National Dairy Council—drink milk; March of Dimes—contributions; Forest Service—do not litter. Or, allow your child to choose the material which he/she wishes to advertise.

Set the time limits. Ten- or fifteen-second spot announcements are the easiest to manage. Have your child create radio commercials using the main idea covered in the commercial. You may even wish to use 3 x 5 assignment cards, with the commercials on "account assignments."

During the playback, ask your child to identify main idea, goals, persuasiveness, creativity, and so on. Compare his/her commercials with the professional commercials. Many times your child's work will be better.

3.   If the local weather bureau has a telephone service which tells the local weather, have your child:

A. Dial the weather service.

B. Listen to the forecast.

C. Use some basic weather instruments or look up the forecast in the local newspaper.

D. Write a script which includes all the information for a short weather announcement (one minute, perhaps two).

E. Record on the cassette recorder an announcement telling what the weather was, what the weather is, and what the weather-caster says the weather will be.

4.   Ask your child to write and produce a one-minute consumer-reporter spot. Various topics may be chosen which tie in to consumerism, e.g.,

—How to buy and choose a product (tomato).

—How to pick a good cucumber.

—How to identify fresh meat.

—How to figure unit pricing.

Encourage your child to use school resources, such as the home economics staff, the science teacher, etc. Contact the local office of the Department of Agriculture for free background material on consumerism. Or call the local office of consumer affairs for free materials. Or write your local congressman for free government publications.

5.   Ask your child to interview a relative (a parent, brother, sister, etc.). You might want to center the interview around a recent family event or a holiday in

order to have a topic for the interview. You may ask your child to choose a community leader to interview for an oral history or social studies topic.

Have your child rehearse the initial questions in advance of the interview. If necessary, coach the child in asking questions. Tape the interview. A family history can be made this way, and kept fully up to date. The taped interview is often an excellent way to memorialize family events, to develop a listening album which will be enjoyed many years later. The tape may also be helpful in solving any problems relative to a family event.

If there is a point of family controversy, the interview technique can spark an analysis of the problem. For example, if there is a controversy between siblings, you (the parent) can make the interview with each child separately and discuss the entire side of the issue. Then, you may do the identical interview with the other disputant. Play back the interviews with both parties present, and move the discussion from there.

USING GAME AND QUIZ SHOWS TO INCREASE LEARNING

For the interval before 8:00 p.m., when network programs begin, most local stations do not air programs of local interest. Generally, local stations do not have enough budget flexibility to produce programs of purely local interest. Rather, they choose to broadcast programs that are acquired through syndication firms, which distribute programs including reruns, documentaries, game shows, and quiz shows. In one week in the Philadelphia area, viewers could choose from among such evening fare as *To Tell the Truth, Name that Tune, $25,000 Pyramid, The Newlywed Game, Hollywood Squares, The Price is Right, Match Game, The $128,000 Question, Family Feud,* and *Tattletales*—not to mention the host of game shows aired during the day. In many cases, Philadelphians could get double and triple doses of the same show on different nights.

Many persons who ordinarily might consider these game and quiz shows trivial and banal could find a goldmine of opportunities to help children learn. There are, of course, many programs that offer no significant information, but merely entertaining gossip. However, many quiz and game shows present an immense series of questions and answers which, if nothing else, bring out interesting facts. A resourceful parent might see that the child participates in the quiz panels, and tries to answer *some* questions before hearing the answers. When the answer is given, the parent can write the topic down; the topic can then provide the impetus for a trip to the nearest dictionary or encyclopedia. What does this do? It ties television viewing to reading, use of the dictionary, practice with the alphabet, pronunciation, and attention to the topic itself.

Parents should not try to over-use TV quiz programs. This will only tend to cause the child to feel too great an intrusion into his television world. However, by occasionally writing down some of the facts, names, questions, and so on, you can design useful and creative follow-up activities from these game shows.

Another technique to employ with your child is to participate with the celebrities. Generally, there is enough time and chatter during the show to permit all members of the family to give their answers before the celebrities or contestants do. This participation, even if it includes guessing, is a learning experience, because when the correct answer is given, family members can corroborate or correct their guesses. The act of participating and waiting to hear the answer involves suspense and insures attention. Sparking the child's attention is critical to encouraging the child to learn.

Competition is part of our way of life. Therefore, some friendly competition among the family, conducted in a spirit of sportsmanship, can be fun. For example, each "home contestant" can keep score on how many correct answers he or she gave during a particular show. If there are wide differences among the family members' knowledge, making comparison unfair, then the scores can be compared in terms of improvement in the number of correct answers over the previous week's totals. For instance, if Johnny had ten correct *Hollywood Square* answers one night, then by giving 12 correct answers the next night he gets an improvement score of two, to be compared with the improvement scores of other family members.

The most important contribution of game shows to learning is that they provide a motivating starting-point. Having identified the interesting items in the television shows, families can use the points of interest to motivate children to learn during trips to the library, work with the dictionary and encyclopedia, and other constructive activities.

10 HOW TO USE TELEVISION TO NURTURE YOUR CHILD'S VALUES AND MORAL DEVELOPMENT

HOW TO USE TELEVISION TO NURTURE YOUR CHILD'S VALUES AND MORAL DEVELOPMENT

Television, more than any other medium or force in our society, has exposed children and adolescents to a wide variety of values, beliefs, attitudes, and lifestyles. Talk shows, news specials, documentaries, children's programs, TV movies, variety programs, quiz programs, soap operas, and commercials all project differing and conflicting sets of values and beliefs about what is worth living for, what we should be, how we should live, what we should own, how society should be organized, and so on. Parents take different approaches to dealing with this opening up of values.

Many parents consciously or unconsciously adopt a laissez-faire "hands-off" attitude toward TV. These parents simply ignore the situation, and let their children watch whatever they like. Most of these parents, I believe, have very little understanding of what effect this laissez-faire attitude has on their children's values development. Young people in our fast-moving and rapidly changing society are confronted with many more choices than in previous generations. They face a bewildering array of alternatives. For example, only a few years ago, women in our society were expected to be housewives, secretaries, teachers, or nurses. These were virtually the only options open to them. Today, it is becoming increasingly more common to meet women doctors, lawyers, dentists, executives, mechanics, and so on. Thus, it is becoming a truism that young people in our society can become whatever they want if they are will to work at it—the means are available.

The problem is, that young people often lack the skills they need to direct their lives through such a confusing maze of options. They simply do not know how to sort through the alternatives and separate what will be good for them from what will be wasteful or harmful. This is not surprising, since children and adolescents left on their own, without any direction, do not develop these skills automatically. Children and adolescents need training in how to make values decisions. the laissez-faire approach to child-rearing simply does not provide them with this training. (See Box 1 for more on this.)

Box 1

Developmental psychologists are learning that the kind of reasoning children must do to arrive at sound value-judgments and moral decisions develops in several sequential stages. For example, a child at an early stage of development will decide what is right and wrong in terms of the immediate personal physical consequences or self-benefit that might occur if a certain choice is made, or a certain action taken. At a later stage, the child makes moral decisions based upon what others think is right or what is defined as right by our society's laws. At a still later stage of development, the child will decide what is right according to what will produce the "greatest good for the greatest number of people," or by ethical principle. A child at an early stage of development will, at the appropriate age, tend to move to the next higher stage of development if exposed to the type of moral reasoning used in the higher stage, and so on for each of the sequential stages. However, if the child is not exposed to a next higher stage of reasoning, he or she may remain stuck at the present stage.[1] Thus, parents who use a laissez-faire attitude as the basis of their child-rearing, and simply allow their children to watch as much television as they want, without ever encouraging their children to discuss the value schemes and moral issues that are inherent in the programs, may well inhibit the natural development of their children's moral reasoning abilities.

Other parents adopt what might be termed an imposition or moralizing approach to their children's TV viewing. Such parents assume that they know what values are best for their children. Thus, programs which expose their children to different values are prohibited. Children and adolescents are allowed to watch only parentally-approved programs with the "right" values. If, by chance, their children are accidently exposed to unapproved values on TV, the parents feel that it is their responsibility to point out how wrong these different values are; thus the child is likely to get a moralistic lecture, especially if he or she shows any inclination of questioning or exploring the different values.

The major defects of this approach are that it prevents children and adolescents from developing an understanding of how people with differing beliefs and values live, and encourages ignorance and intolerance of other ways of life. It also prevents children from learning to think for themselves, and thus does not provide them with the decision-making skills that they will need as they approach adulthood.

The imposition approach to child-rearing is often highly effective with young children if the goal is to produce "approved" behavior, but it becomes less effective as the child reaches adolescence. For one thing, adolescents begin to resent the control exerted upon them by parents, and thus, at the first opportunity, they often rebel against parental domination by rejecting the values that Mom and Dad have imposed. This is particularly likely to happen where the parents have demanded a role—obedience to their values, without attempting to acquaint their children with the reasons behind their adoption of those values, and without letting the child discover what may result from the espousal of a different set of values. I have seen many college freshmen and sophomores take the exact opposite views from their parents, because they resent what they consider arbitrary restrictions and attitudes imposed by their parents.

The most damaging effect of this approach, however, is not realized until adolescents reach the age when they must begin to make their own decisions. Never having learned to think on their own, they must either constantly turn to others to make decisions for them, or feel confused and overwhelmed by the world that surrounds them.

Still other parents adopt a third approach, which we shall term a values-clarification approach to childrearing. Parents using this approach allow their children to watch TV programs which expose the children to a wide range of values, beliefs, attitudes, and lifestyles. (With young children, programs such as horror and murder shows are restricted because of harmful effects they may have on the child's psychological and emotional development.) Then, the parent takes an active role in helping the child or adolescent to think about the consequences of holding and acting on these various beliefs, values, and attitudes. This is usually done in one of three ways. One way is to ask the child some clarifying questions, either after the TV program or during the commercial break, which help the child think through the values issues involved. The second way is to use one of the values activities or games developed by Simon, *et.al.*,[2] following the conclusion of the TV program, to help the child reflect on the values issues involved. The third way is to set aside a time each week to pose a values question or dilemma, or use a value game or activity to help the child explore the various values issues invariably raised by TV programs.

The first two methods require the parent to watch the TV programs with the child, so that appropriate questions can be formulated, while the third method can be used at any time, without the parent having viewed the same TV program as the child. The aim of all three methods is to help children and adolescents think through the values issues involved, and to arrive at their own freely-chosen values. More specifically, the questions and activities are intended to help children:

1. Identify the values issue(s) involved in the program.

2. Think through the values issue(s) by:

   a. gathering more data.

   b. considering alternatives.

   c. predicting and weighing consequences (both personal and social).

3. Formulate a stand or point of view on the issue(s).

4. Affirm the stand or point of view by:

   a. sharing it with others.

   b. making a public statement when appropriate.

5. Set goals and/or plan how to act on their stand or point of view.

6. Act upon their values.

7. Evaluate the impact and effectiveness of their actions.

The assumption behind this approach is, that if children learn and use this seven-step process to formulate their own values, these values will more likely to be sound ones that will hold up over time than those values which have been imposed by parents and other authority figures, or haphazardly acquired as a result of unevaluated experience. Moreover, children will develop a decision-making process which they can use for the rest of their lives to formulate and reformulate values in our rapidly changing society. Finally, the approach is consistent with the natural developmental process undergone by children and adolescents in learning to think at increasingly higher levels of moral reasoning. In fact, I believe, that the seven-step valuing process is very likely to facilitate this growth, especially if used in a family setting with children who are at various stages of moral reasoning.

Now let's turn our attention to exploring the three methods of applying the approach.

Method One

In using method one, the parent views the TV program along with the child. Then, at an appropriate time, either during a commercial break or at the conclusion of the program (or some later point), the parent asks the child one or several clarifying questions aimed at helping the child examine and think about the value and moral issues raised by the program.

Below are plot summaries from several different popular television programs. Following each plot summary are a number of values-clarifying questions that parents might ask their children upon conclusion of the program or during a commercial break. (In our family, we usually prefer to wait until the program is finished rather than trying to sandwich a values discussion in between commercial breaks.) I have included a greater number of questions than parents would actually want to ask, to give an indication of the kinds of questions that can be used to help children explore value issues. In actual practice, only one or two of the sample questions for each program would be used.

The Little House On The Prairie *Plot Summary*

In this episode, the Ingalls inherit a large amount of money. They soon find themselves besieged by requests to donate money for a church organ and to buy books for the school library. They are also treated very differently now by the townspeople. In the end, the inheritance is eaten up by legal fees, and the Ingalls almost lose their farm because of the large debts they have incurred by spending the inheritance money before they actually received it.

Values-Clarifying Questions:

1. If you suddenly inherited a large amount of money, how would you use it?

2. If someone wanted to be your friend just because you were rich, what would you do?

3. What is the most important thing you consider in choosing a friend?

4. If you had been one of the townspeople who could have bought the Ingalls farm for three cents, would you have given the farm back to them?

Happy Days *Plot Summary*

In this episode, Fonzie tries to convince Chachi that a gang member's life is not as "cool" as it looks.

Values-Clarifying Questions:

1. If your two best friends joined a gang that did things that you didn't like to do, would you join the gang to keep up the friendships, or not join and risk losing your two friends?

2. What would you do if you met a new kid whom you really liked, but for some reason, the rest of your gang didn't want him to join them?

3. Suppose your gang began doing something which you consider wrong; if you object, they will kick you out of the gang. What would you do?

The Brady Bunch *Plot Summary*

Marsha breaks a date when the most popular boy in the school asks her out. He decides, however, to break the date with her when he learns that she has broken her nose, and because of the swelling in her face, is no longer very attractive.

Values-Clarifying Questions:

1. Would you break a date to be able to go out with the most popular boy in your school?

2. What is most important to you in choosing a boyfriend or a girlfriend? Attractiveness? Personality? Popularity? Loyalty? Other things? What?

3. If someone broke a date with you to go out with the most popular person in school, what would you do?

Special on Martin Luther King

This three-part series portrays the life of Martin Luther King, from his early years in the ministry to his death.

Values-Clarifying Questions:

1. Is there anything you believe in so strongly that you would risk your reputation or life to stand up for it?

2. If you had been a young adult at the time of the Selma demonstration, would you have wanted to march with Martin Luther King?

3. Have you ever been in a situation in which you or your friends have been discriminated against? What did you do?

4. Where do you stand on the use of force to bring

about social change? Are you closer to Martin Luther King, who believed in non-violence, or to Malcolm X, who believed that force should be met with force?

5. Would you invite a close friend of another race or religion to a party even if others at the party would reject you for doing so?

James At 16 *Plot Summary*

James makes friends with a new kid at school, who is allowed to do whatever he wants. James's parents, however, have rules and regulations which require James to be home at a certain time, do his homework, and so on. They insist that James bring his new friend to dinner so that the family can meet him. Surprisingly, James discovers that his new friend wishes he had a family more like James's family.

Values-Clarifying Questions:

1. Do you think you should be allowed, as a teenager, to go whereever and do whatever you want without parental permission?

2. When you become a parent and have a teenager, what rules and regulations will you set for him/her? Why?

The goal of the above questions is not to instill a particular set of values, but rather to help children and adolescents to develop the skills they need to formulate and reformulate their own values, now and in the future. To accomplish this, the parent uses questions and other activities to help children to:

1. Become aware of the beliefs and behaviors that they prize and are willing to stand up for.

2. Consider alternative modes of thinking and acting.

3. Weigh the pros and cons and the consequences of various alternatives.

4. Select the most sound course of action and act upon it.

5. Consider whether their actions match their stated beliefs, and if not, how they can bring the two into closer harmony.

To accomplish these goals, it is vitally important that you follow several guidelines in using the approach. In my work with parents and teachers, I invariably discover that when children fail to respond to a values question, or to get involved in a values activity, it is because the parent or teacher is violating one or more of the following guidelines:

1. Be accepting and non-judgmental of your child's responses. Nothing kills values exploration quicker than verbal or non-verbal indications on your part that you are looking for and willing to accept only "right" answers. Do not use values questions or activities to moralize, or to teach your child "correct" values.

2. Respect and demand that other family members

respect, the rights of your child to have his or her own feelings and views. Always allow your child to pass on any question or on part of any activity, or not to participate at all if he or she so chooses.

3. Respect and protect the confidentiality of your child's responses. Insist that discussions remain a family matter, and that personal information not be talked about outside of the family unless permission to do so is secured from all parties.

4. Participate in the activities yourself. Let your child have a say first, then share your views. If you do so non-judgmentally, your child will probably be very interested in how you came to feel or think as you do. On the other hand, if your child feels that you are trying to *make a point*, then he or she will probably be more interested in defending himself or herself than in listening to your views.

Method Two

In method two, the parent must also view the TV program along with the child, but instead of asking clarifying questions to stimulate discussion, the parent uses a values activity or game to structure the child's values exploration. In the next few pages, I will demonstrate how two of the values strategies developed by Simon, Kirschenbaum, and Howe for classroom use can be adapted and used by parents to nurture children's values development. As you will see, most of the examples I use can be related to a wide variety of specific TV programs and incidents. Thus, the examples should serve to give you an idea how you can make up your own TV-related "Voting Questions," and "Rank Orders." For more on how to adapt the values-clarification strategies, Dr. Simon has coauthored a book entitled, *Helping Your Child Learn Right From Wrong*,[3] in which he demonstrates how many of the values-clarification activities can be used in the family setting.

Box 2

The research that has been done on the values-clarification approach indicates that children who have been exposed to this approach:

"have become less apathetic, less flighty, less conforming as well as less over-dissenting. They are more zestful and energetic, more critical in their thinking, and more likely to follow through on decisions. In the case of underachievers, values clarification has led to better success in school."[4]

VALUES RANKING

This activity gives children practice in choosing from alternatives and publicly affirming and explaining their choices. It also helps children see that many issues require more thoughtful consideration than they tend to give them.

To use the activity, explain that you are going to ask some questions, following a TV program, which will require thoughtful consideration. If there is more than one child in the family, each child will be allowed to answer the question by ranking several alternatives (stating his or her first choice, second choice, and so on), and then explaining his or her ranking. When the children have finished sharing their rankings, then share *your* rankings and the reasons for them.

Here are some examples:

1. Following a program in which one of the characters inherits a large sum of money, the parent asks, "If you suddenly inherited a good deal of money, what would you do?"

   a. Put it in a savings bank.

   b. Spend it on something for yourself.

   c. Invest it in land or in stocks and bonds.

   Additional items: *

   a. Give it to charity or some other good cause.

   b. Buy something for someone else.

   c. Take a trip.

2. During a commercial break in a children's program about friendship, the parent asks, "Which do you consider most important in choosing a friend?"

---

*Present only three rank-order items. This is about all children can handle at one time. Use the additional items as second set of rank orders, or as substitutions.

a. Good looks.

b. Personality.

c. Loyalty.

Additional items:

a. Honesty.

b. Intelligence.

c. Generosity.

3. Following a program in which one of the main characters receives a birthday gift that she doesn't like, the parents ask, "What would you want someone to do if you gave him/her a gift he/she didn't like?"

a. Keep the gift and thank you politely.

b. Tell you politely that he or she doesn't like it.

c. Return the gift to the store without telling you.

4. Following a news special on problems in the city, the parent asks, "Which do you consider the most serious problem in our city today?"

a. Poverty and unemployment.

b. Crime.

c. Racial discrimination.

Additional items:

a. Pollution.

b. Transportation.

c. Taxes.

5. Following a program in which the hero tries to decide what he wants to do with his life, the parent asks, "Which do you think is most important?"

a. To make lots of money.

b. To have lots of friends.

c. To be free to do whatever you want, when you want.

Additional items:

a. To be famous.

b. To be very wise.

6. Following a news special on marriage and divorce in the United States, the parent asks, "Which is most important in the selection of a mate?"

a. Personality.

b. Physical attractiveness.

c. Money.

Additional items:

a. Intelligence.

b. Family background.

Or, "Which would bother you the most in your mate?"

    a. Talks too much.

    b. Smokes too much.

    c. Drinks too much.

Additional items:

    a. Leaves the house too messy.

    b. Spends too much money.

7. Following a program entitled *A Closer Look At Our Schools,* the parent asks, "What do you consider to be the most serious problem in your school?"

    a. Discipline.

    b. Drugs.

    c. Apathy.

8. Following a news special on problems today, the parent asks, "If you were head of a funding agency, which of the following would receive the highest priority?"

    a. Medical research.

    b. Education.

    c. Poverty programs.

Additional items:

    a. National defense.

    b. Space program.

Or, "What do you consider to be the most pressing problem facing our society?"

a. Economy (inflation/recession).

b. Air, water, and noise pollution.

c. Race and sex discrimination.

Additional items:

a. Over-population.

b. Transportation.

c. Inequitable distribution of wealth.

d. Crime.

Or, "Which of the following do you think is having the most harmful effect in our society?"

a. "Hard" drugs, like heroin.

b. Marijuana.

c. Alcohol.

Additional items:

a. Cigarettes.

b. Food additives and preservatives.

c. Prescription drugs, like barbituates, amphetamines, etc.

VALUES VOTING

This activity is a simple way to raise values issues with children. It helps them begin to identify and think about where they stand on various values issues, as well as giving them a chance to publicly affirm their beliefs.

Following a program, or during a commercial break, the parent raises one or several values issues with the words, "How many here. . .?" (with one child the phrase, "Do you. . .?" may be substituted). For example, following a program in which the issue of honesty is raised, the parent might ask, "How many here think that telling white lies is ever justified?" The children then raise their hands if they agree, put their thumbs down if they disagree, or fold their arms if they are neutral on the issue. The parent should vote slightly after children, so as to not influence their votes. Discussion can then follow, with everyone explaining his or her vote.

Here are some examples of values issues raised on TV and values-voting questions which could be used to explore them. Each question below should be prefaced by the statement, "How many here. . .?" or "Do you. . . .?"

TV Program/Incident:	Values-Voting Question:
1. Religious program.	. . .think it's important to attend religious services regularly?
2. Family show in which one of the children is not doing his chores, so his parents cut off his allowance.	. . .think children should have to work for their allowance?

3. Program on political   . . .would like to go into
    campaigns.   politics someday?

4. Program on women's rights.   . . .think women with young
                                     children should work full
                                     time?

5. Program on world   . . .would vote for a law to
    population explosion.   limit the size of families to
                                     two children?

6. Family show in which an   . . .think it is right for
    older sister is left to babysit   older brothers and sisters
    her younger brother.   to discipline younger ones?

7. Baseball game.   . . .would rather play in a
                                     baseball game than watch
                                     one?

8. Family show in which the   . . .think it is right for girls
    girls play dolls and the boys   to play with Hot Wheels
    play with a racing set.   racing sets?

                                   . . .think it right for boys
                                     to play with Barbie Dolls?

9. Program on choosing a
    career.   . . .would change to a job
                                     you didn't like if it offered
                                     you a lot more money?

10. Program on drug abuse.   . . .would turn in your best
                                     friend for selling illegal
                                     drugs?

Method Three

In method three, the parent does not view TV with the child, but rather finds time each week to do one or more activities designed to raise values issues. Once the values issues are identified, the parent can then help the child clarify his or her values by considering other alternatives, weighing consequences of holding different points of view, exploring patterns of action, and so on. In this way, values and attitudes to which the child was exposed via TV can surface and be explored.

The following is a brief list of method-three activities which you can use to help your child identify and think through the various values issues. For a much more extensive listing, and for a detailed description of these and other values-clarification activities, see *Values Clarification: A Handbook* by Simon, Howe and Kirschenbaum, and *Personalizing Education: Values Clarification and Beyond* by Howe and Howe available from Hart Publishing Co., 12 East 12th Street, New York, N.Y. 10003 or from the Philadelphia Center for Humanistic Education, 8504 Germantown Ave., Phila., Pa. 19118. (Also See Chapter 15).

Activities For Getting Clear
1. Have your child make a values collage by cutting out pictures of his favorite things from magazines and pasting them on a large sheet of paper. Post the collage and then discuss it.

2. Tell your child to pretend that he/she is going on a trip to a distant land where people still live without modern conveniences: electricity, etc. The child can take only one suitcase. Ask the child to make a list of the things he/she would pack. Then, have him/her discuss the list.

3. Have your child build a paper memorial to a

person, place, thing, or idea which he/she holds in high esteem. First, he/she is to make a list of people, ideas, etc., to which the memorial might be dedicated. Give the child a stack of newspapers and a roll of masking tape, and tell him/her to build a paper tower as a memorial. *Variation:* Family members can build a group memorial.

4. Tell your child to pretend that he/she has been asked to make a time capsule, which will be opened 500 years from now, to let people know what our times were really like. Have the child make a list of five things about our society which he/she likes or values, and five things about our society which he/she dislikes or is against.

5. Have your child plan a family vacation. First, the child should make a list of all the places he/she would like to go, and things he/she would like to do. Then, provide the child with certain constraints, like budget, time, etc., and have him/her plan the vacation in detail.

6. Have your child make a list of hopes for the future and regrets that the past. Give the child a chance to share his/her list with the family.

7. At the dinner table or family gathering, have each family member share something of which he or she is proud. You might want to consider making this a family ritual. For variation, give a specific focus, like, "Share something about the family of

which you are proud," or, "Tell about something that you have done for someone of which you are proud."

8. Ask your child to pretend that he/she has been given a disposable computer which is capable of answering any *one* question fed into it. After that, the computer must be thrown away. The child's task is to make a list of the most important questions he/she can think of that need answering. Then, the child is to select the one single most important question to be asked.

9. Have your child make a list of all the ways he/she can think of to spend his/her free time. Then, the child is to rank-order the list. Help the child make plans to begin doing the things he/she really likes to do.

10. Have your child plan a holiday celebration. Some things to consider are food, decorations, rituals, entertainment, guest list, and gifts. *Variations:* Have your child plan a party or festival to celebrate a person, an event, or an idea.

11. Tell your child to pretend that he/she had been granted three wishes, which will all come true. Have your child share the three wishes and why they are important with the family.

12. Give your child some newspapers and magazines and ask him/her to cut out headlines and stories

that raise important values issues (e.g., ecology, abortion, welfare, women's rights, etc.). These can be attached to newsprint and posted. The child can then rank the headlines and stories, from most important to think about and deal with to least important. Have him/her discuss the values issues in the stories and talk about what should be done, what alternatives might be considered, what the consequences of various actions and positions might be, etc.

13. Have your child make a list of favorite heroes and heroines. Then, give the child a chance to explain why he/she values each of the heroes and heroines on the list.

14. Have your child design a dream house. Where would it be built? What would it look like? How big would it be? What would be put in it?

15. Tell your child to make a list of all the electrical appliances around the house, including the TV, hi fi, etc. When the list is finished, tell the child to pretend that there is a brown-out, and that he or she must get rid of three things on the list. The child must decide what will go. Now tell the child the brown-out is getting worse; he or she must get rid of three more things. Continue this until three or fewer items remain on the list.

16. Have your child go on a scavenger hunt around the neighborhood. The child is to find five things

of beauty and five things which are not so beautiful in the neighborhood. Have the child share his or her findings with the family.

17. Tell your child to pretend that he or she has just been given a magic box which can contain whatever he or she wants to be in it. The child is to share what will be in his/her magic box. *Variation:* Have your child pretend that he or she has been given a magic carpet which will go any place in the world.

18. Have your child keep a values diary, or make an "All About Me" book. Each day, the child is to write about something important that has happened to him or her, something that he or she has achieved or done for someone, a stand taken, a feeling about some issue, and so on. This is to be a private diary or book, to be shared only if the child wishes to share it.

19. Have your child prepare and then give a five-minute autobiography. The autobiography should stress the significant events and people that have affected the child.

20. Ask your child to make a list of places to go, things to do or read, people to visit or talk to that would help sensitize him or her to the important values issues of our time. For example, to sensitize the child to the problems of the aging, he or she might visit a retirement home or nursing home,

and talk with some of the residents about what their life there is like.

21. Have your child make a list of all the things he/she is for and a second list of all the things he/she is against. Discuss the list.

22. Ask your child to complete the sentence, "I prefer _____ to _____." For example, "I prefer *the country* to *the city.*" This can be repeated several times, or until the child tires of it. *Variation:* Use the sentence, "I'd rather be a _____ than a _____."

23. Have your child complete the sentence stem, "I wonder. . . ." For exmple, "I wonder why some people hate other people of a different skin color when they don't even know them?" Then, help the child find ways to get answers to these questions.

24. Have your child make a list of all the people, jobs, and organizations that are needed to make the world go. Then, have the child choose the five most important factors and explain their significance.

25. Have your child write a want ad in which he or she tells about something he or she wants or is seeking.

26. Have your child think about something he/she would like to be (an animal, a celebrity, a bird)

and to transform the phrase "If I were a
_____ I would. . . ." into a very brief story.

27. Pose a *this or that* problem, and ask your child
which he/she is more like. For example, "Are you
more like ping-pong ball or a paddle?" Or, "Are
you more like a row-boat or a cabin-cruiser?"
Then, have the child explain his/her answer.

28. Have your child design a greeting card to send to
friends, with the most important message the child
can think of written inside.

29. Ask your child to make a list of all the important
character traits (honesty, cheerfulness, in-
dependence, etc.) that he/she thinks a person
needs to be successful and happy in our society.
Then, have the child rank-order the list from most
important to least important, and discuss. *Variation:* Have your child make a list of values, (i.e.,
freedom, truth, beauty, friendship, etc.) which are
worth living for, rank-order it, and discuss.

30. Have your child write a story with a moral, and
discuss.

31. Ask your child to make a list of favorite things
about school, and another list of detested things
about school. Then have the child discuss the lists.

SPEAKING OUT ACTIVITIES

Once your child is clear about what he or she is for and against, encourage him or her to speak out and take action. This is what it takes to make a free and democratic government like ours work. Here are some ideas for helping your child learn to speak out.

Encourage your child to:

1. Write a letter to the editor of the local newspaper.

2. Design posters which speak out, and to post them in public buildings. *Variation:* Design a bumper sticker.

3. Design a button with an appropriate slogan, and wear it.

4. Write a letter or send a telegram to government representatives or officials urging them to take action on some issue.

5. Send an "I urge. . . ." telegram to any person who might respond, and urge that individual to get involved.

6. Design and pass out flyers or leaflets which speak to some issue.

7. Develop and carry out a door-to-door campaign

on a specific issue, urging neighbors and friends to get involved. *Variation:* Conduct a telephone campaign.

8. Write a petition, get people to sign it, and then send it to the appropriate officials.

9. Write a guest editorial and try to get it published in the editorial section of a magazine or newspaper.

10. Set up a soap-box on a busy street-corner or some other public place, and speak to anyone that will listen.

11. Organize a speakout, to be held as a separate event or in conjunction with some other gathering. People are to take turns speaking out on a specific issue.

12. Use time at family gatherings to speak out on some issue.

13. Organize and hold a real or mock demonstration on some issue of concern.

14. Make speeches to community organizations, women's groups, etc. Many such groups are always looking for speakers.

15. Develop and publish a local newsletter to speak out and keep people informed.

16. Call in on one of the local radio talk shows and speak out on some issue of concern.

Footnotes

[1]Duska, Ronald and Mariellen Wheelan, *Moral Development: A Guide To Piaget and Kohlberg*, Paulist Press, New York, 1975.

[2]Simon, Sidney B., Leland W. Howe, and Howard Kirschenbaum, *Values Clarification: A Handbook*, Hart Publishing Co., New York, 1972.

[3]Simon, Sidney B., and Sally Wendkos Olds, *Helping Your Child Learn Right From Wrong*, Simon & Schuster, New York, 1976.

[4]Raths, Louis, Merrill Harmin, and Sidney B. Simon, *Values and Teaching*, Charles Merrill Publishing Co., Columbus, Ohio, 1964.

11 HOW TO ANSWER YOUR CHILD'S TV QUESTIONS

HOW TO ANSWER YOUR CHILD'S TV QUESTIONS

TV raises a host of questions for children. Some of these questions are easy to answer, and some of them are not so easy to answer. It is the questions that are difficult to answer that we want to examine here. Questions like, "Why do people die? Am I going to die? Why do people call each other names? What do boys expect from girls?" Such questions often contain more than the child's simple desire to know more about his or her world. Usually, these questions arise from the child's concern about his or her identity—"who am I?" questions—or from the child's concern about his or her relationship with others, or from the child's concern about his or her ability to control and influence others and the environment. These questions are often the child's way of letting parents know that he or she is fearful or emotionally upset about something. Factual answers to these questions do not provide the kind of help the child is seeking. Rather, they often serve to compound the child's problem, since he or she may begin to feel that nobody understands or cares.

Unfortunately, we parents often listen only to the child's words, instead of to both the child's words and the child's feelings. Thus, we may give a factual answer to a feeling question, which then leaves the child still upset. The key to differentiating between questions in which the child simply wants information, and questions in which the child is seeking a chance to express his or her concerns and fears and solve the problem he or she faces, is to listen for the feeling message. Information questions will contain little or no feeling message. Concern questions, on the other hand, will be loaded with feelings. Information questions should be answered simply and in a straightforward manner, by giving the child the information that he or she seeks. Not so for concern questions; they require a different kind of response. We call this response *reflective listening*.

Reflective listening (or active listening as it is often called, to differentiate it from passive listening) reflects back to the child the listener's understanding of both the child's words and the child's feelings. Reflective listening lets the child know that his or her concerns, fears, anger, embarrassment, or sorrow has been heard and understood. Knowing this, the child can go on to express more of his or her feelings. Again, the listener reflects or feeds back his or her understanding of what the child feels and has said. This continues until the child has fully expressed his or her concerns, fears, anxiety, frustrations, etc., and is no longer upset by them, or until the child arrives at his or her own solution to the problem he or she is facing.

Note that this method is based upon the assumption that children can and will solve their own problems if parents listen. Too often, we parents try to solve problems for our children by giving them advice, making suggestions, lecturing them, analyzing their problems, directing them, and so on. These methods often serve to undermine the child's faith in his or her own ability to deal with a personal problem, and thus tend to make the child more dependent upon us.

Following is a brief dialogue between a mother and daughter, in which the mother uses reflective listening to help her daughter think through and resolve a personal concern.

Daughter: (following a TV show in which a teenage couple decide that going steady is not what they really want) What do boys want from girls like me?

Mother: Sounds like you are wondering what kind of a relationship boys want with you?

Daughter: Yeah. I feel kind of mixed-up about it.

Mother: You're feeling confused about your relationship with boys?

Daughter: I guess so. I mean, I like to kiss and all that, but boys always want more!

Mother: It upsets you that boys want more than kisses from you.

Daughter: Yes. And sometimes I want to do more than kiss, but I know it's dangerous. I know the right thing to do, but it is very hard because the boys get mad at me.

Mother: It is hard to do what you believe is right, because you don't enjoy having boys being angry with you. And your inner conflicts complicate the problem even more.

Daughter: That's right. I want boys to like me. I want to be happy. But I couldn't be happy if I didn't like myself, and I can't like myself if I don't do what I think is right.

Mother: You want boys to like you, and you want to be happy, but your happiness is largely based on self-respect.

Daughter: You know, the more I think about it, any boy who doesn't like me because I do what I think is right isn't worth having as a boyfriend. And I guess I have to subject biological urges to higher priorities. Thanks, Mom. Well, I've got lots of homework to do.

Note that the mother did not try to solve her daughter's concern by giving her advice or making suggestions, nor did she preach or lecture her on sexual morality. She did not fly off the handle when her daughter confessed to "biological urges." The mother simply listened and reflected back her daughter's thoughts and feelings. Her daughter did the rest. You can be sure that if the mother were the kind of mother who felt obliged to solve her daughter's problems for her, or to lecture her on sexual morality, her daughter would never have raised the concern with her in the first place. Instead, she would have kept it to herself, or talked with her friends about it. Very few parents really know their children's fears, concerns, and problems. they are too busy trying to shape and discipline them to really help them. And they are too quick to idealize their own childhood or adolescence, and to forget that they experienced many of the same conflicts as their children.

Learning to listen and feed back to your child what you hear, without interpreting, analyzing, or giving advice, is a difficult skill. It will require a sound understanding of the reflective listening process—its goals and how it works—and lots of practice in reflective listening. To help you learn the skill, we suggest that you do the following:

1.   Buy Thomas Gordon's book, *Parent Effectiveness Training*, which is available in paperback bookstores or from The Philadelphia Humanistic Education Center, 8504 Germantown Ave., Phila., Pa. 19118. This book is loaded with information on effective parenting methods, including a large section on how to use reflective listening with children.

2.   Enroll in a Parent Effectiveness Training class led by a certified P.E.T. teacher. You will learn how to

use reflective listening and how to solve any problems you encounter in using reflective listening with your own family. For information on P.E.T. classes in your local area, write:

> Effectiveness Training
> Peter H. Wyden/Publisher
> 750 Third Avenue
> New York, N.Y. 10017

3.   Try taking the quiz below. It will help you assess your understanding of reflective listening. If you do well on the quiz, then try writing down some typical comments that your own children might make, and see if you can come up with a reflective-listening response which does not evaluate, support, interpret, or probe. If you do poorly on the quiz, buy the *Parent Effectiveness Training* book and study it, and/or enroll in a P.E.T. class.

4.   Before using reflective listening with your children, try practicing the techniques on your spouse or on a friend. Ask them to talk about a problem or concern of theirs, and then see if you can reflect back what you hear. Follow these guidelines:

A.   Do not evaluate what they say and feel or make judgmental responses.

B.   Do not interpret or analyze what they say or feel.

C.   Do not try to be supportive by saying how you feel or saying that you agree with what they say or feel.

D. Do not talk about your own experiences or feelings, even if you have faced the same problem or concern and solved it successfully.

E. Do not give advice or suggestions as to how the person can solve his or her problem unless he or she asks for it.

F. Do not ask questions to try to find out the person's reasons or motivation for doing or thinking something.

A REFLECTIVE LISTENING QUIZ

Instructions: Read each of the following comments and circle the response below it that comes the closest to what you think a reflective-listening reponse should be. Then, consult the key on page 160 to check your answers.

1. "Why do some people talk all the time when they have nothing to say! It makes me angry. I wish they would just shut up. They're only trying to impress people."

A. You shouldn't be so critical of others.

B. You think some people talk a lot because they have an inferiority complex.

C. I know how you feel.

D. It upsets you to hear someone talk about something when you feel they are trying to impress others with their talk.

    E. Do you think it's wrong to try to impress others?

2. "I always seem to do the wrong thing. I'm just a jerk."

    A. You feel like the worst person in the whole world.

    B. How long have you felt like a jerk?

    C. You feel you never do anything right.

    D. I feel that way sometimes too.

    E. You shouldn't run yourself down.

3. "Just leave me alone! I don't want to talk with anyone, do anything with anybody. No one cares about me."

    A. I felt just like that one time.

    B. That's a stupid thing to say.

    C. You're upset and want to be left alone because no one cares about you.

    D. Has someone hurt you recently?

    E. You feel that people hate you.

4. "I don't want to play with him anymore. He's a dummy, and he's selfish and mean."

    A. You are afraid of him, so you don't want to play with him anymore.

    B. It isn't nice to call someone a dummy.

    C. You're angry with him because you feel he's selfish and mean.

D. If he's selfish and mean, then you don't have to play with him.

E. What did you do to him to make him selfish and mean?

Key

1.		2.		3.		4.	
A.	E	A.	I	A.	S	A.	I
B.	I	B.	P	B.	E	B.	E
C.	S	C.	R	C.	R	C.	R
D.	R	D.	S	D.	P	D.	S
E.	P	E.	E	E.	I	E.	P

E = Evaluative response: A response that classifies and places some kind of a label on another's thoughts and feelings.

S = Supportive response: A response which attempts to show your support of another's comments either through agreement or sharing your own feelings.

I = Interpretive response: A response that goes beyond what the person said and attempts to place him/her in a position in which he/she may not feel he/she belongs.

P = Probing response: A response which attempts to find the person's reason(s) for thinking and feeling as he/she does.

R =   Reflective-listening response: A response
which reflects back to the person what
he/she has said and feels without trying to
go beyond the statement, investigate it, or
label it.

12 HOW TO USE TELEVISION IN THE CLASSROOM: A GUIDE FOR TEACHERS AND PARENTS

Many people, especially educators, consider television to be an enemy of children. They claim that television casts a spell, which, every day after school, somewhat mystically, pulls children into its power, and, except for a quick dinner break, keeps them under its control until they go to sleep. In too many households, unfortunately, this seems to be the pattern. Naturally, teachers will be skeptical when told that it is possible for tremendous learning gains to be realized through the use of commercial television programs. Nevertheless, it is true.

Increasingly, popular television programs are being used in the classroom to help children and adolescents master basic learning, thinking, and valuing skills. For example, Prime Time Television, a non-profit organization in Chicago, has provided over 200,000 teachers with kits designed to help them coordinate classroom instruction with popular, prime-time television programs. Students view the assigned television programs at home; then, teacher-led discussions follow the next day in the classroom. Topics which have been covered to date include violence, conflict, family relationships, stereotyping, hero worship, how to interpret news, law enforcement, criminal justice, politics, and economics.

In Philadelphia, an even more exciting classroom application of television has been developed. Michael P. Marcase, Superintendent of Schools, is leading the nation in raising reading levels through the use of the Television Reading Program. Founded by Dr. Marcase, along with Dr. Bernard Solomon (this book's coauthor), and Michael McAndrew, the Philadelphia School System is pioneering the first thoroughly comprehensive experiments in using television scripts and videotapes to teach children to read. Popular television scripts such as *Sanford and Son, The Rookies,* and *Bewitched* are used as the primary source of reading material in lieu of traditional materials. All the trappings of traditional reading techniques, such as scope and sequence, competencies, teachers' guides, exercises, and tests, have been developed, using the students' favorite television programs. Many classrooms have been equipped with videotape recorders which allow children, each of whom is provided with a script of the videotaped program, to read along with their favorite TV stars. The teacher can stop the action, discuss what is happening, teach or review a basic reading skill, do instant replays, answer student questions, and so on.

Superintendent Marcase has expanded the program into dozens of schools in Philadelphia, and in each case, he found the same results. Children were demanding more scripts to read. Children were taking scripts home and reading them with their families. Children were finally motivated to learn to read—and read they did! Incredible reading gains resulted. Some children made several years advancement in a matter of a few months. Many children skipped three or more years in reading levels during the school year. In Mount Vernon, New York, where the Philadelphia Project was tested with 28 students to determine the impact, more than half the students gained two years or more in reading levels during the five-month testing period. Nearly 90 percent of the students showed marked improvement in reading skills. Reading levels of minority students were raised from low percentiles to the national norm. The Philadelphia Reading Project proved a basic notion about human nature: If a person wants to do something very much, he/she will, most likely, succeed.

Reading experts flew into Philadelphia by the droves to find out more about this very unusual technique. Generally, a brief visit resulted in reading supervisors returning home with sample materials to try in their own systems. As expected, gains in reading were replicated in dozens of cities across the country. The Philadelphia Project has been so successful, that to date at least 3,500 other U.S. school systems are now using a similar approach.

Why does the Philadelphia Project approach work? Simple: motivation! The captivating brilliance of television and its stars was transferred into a useful tool to motivate children to learn. Children acted out the parts of their favorite stars. They became the star. They related to television. Television, with all its blatant materialism and commercialism, helped children learn to read. What irony, this technical marvel of banality was turning non-readers into readers, non-achievers into students, and drop-outs into attendees.

Not content to rest on their laurels, Marcase and his colleagues next applied their concept to the creation of a public-television reading series. If videotapes and scripts did so well in the classroom, they reasoned, then it should be possible to reach millions through the actual broadcast of television reading-oriented material. To implement this concept, a television series was made called *The Reading Show—The Vanishing Shadow*. *The Reading Show* used an old time Saturday-matinee serial entitled *The Vanishing Shadow*, vintage 1930s. The program had enough of a story-line to lend itself to editing. The serial was redone technically with subtitles based on reading comprehension and vocabulary skills. The action was frozen. Instant replay, slow-motion, fast-action, and a host of visual techniques were added to make the serial more entertaining while relating to learning skills. Then, scripts and materials were given to school children in the cities where *The Reading Show* was broadcast.

As usual, the children improved their reading after watching the television serial at home and following up with materials in the classroom. Incidentally, in every city which aired the series, the television station realized a gain in ratings over other stations, and an increase over their regularly-scheduled programming. This is an incredible track record, especially since *The Reading Show* was broadcast during prime access time (7:30 to 8:00 p.m.). The concept of the show was endorsed by the National Education Association, and the series received an award from the highly respected Action for Childrens Television organization. (See sample script for *The Reading Show*, p. 172.)

Another innovation was developed after Marcase negotiated the use of scripts to programs such as *Eleanor and Franklin*. This time, however, the daily newspaper printed the scripts as a supplement, and the entire viewing area joined in the largest reading lesson in history. One hundred and fifty-thousand scripts were printed in the newspaper, and given to the junior and senior high schools in Philadelphia. Hundreds of thousands of additional scripts were made available in the daily newspaper to anyone who paid the 15 cents for the paper. This gave the entire tri-state area (Pennsylvania, New Jersey, and Delaware) the opportunity to read along with the television broadcast and have follow-up discussions at home. This "in advance of broadcast" use of scripts sparked tremendous interest, increased viewers, and increased the role of newspapers in the learning process. Here, everyone gained; especially, the children.

HOW TO USE TELEVISION IN THE CLASSROOM

The following step-by-step guides can be used by teachers and parent-aides in the classroom to plan and teach lessons and units based upon popular television programs. Also, the guides can be used by parents in the home, to supplement their children's regular classroom instruction. We have included three different step-by-step guides. The first guide is designed to help you plan and teach a lesson based upon a popular television program that most of the students in the class have viewed. The second guide is designed to help you develop a unit based upon several episodes of one or more popular television programs. The third guide is designed to help you implement the Philadelphia Schools Television Reading Program in your classroom.

GUIDE 1: CREATING AND TEACHING A TELEVISION LESSON

The following step-by-step lesson planning-teaching process can be used to create a classroom lesson designed to help students explore social and values issues raised by a popular television program. Students need not have viewed the program to participate in the lesson; however, the effectiveness of the lesson is increased if most or all of the students have viewed the program.

Step 1: Select a popular television program which A) students will be able to view (probably a prime-time program), B) raises important social and values issues; e.g., money, crime, women's rights, race relations, inflation, drug abuse, political corruption, and C) is free of violence, sexism, racism, and "put-downs"—unless these are the issues to be studied.

(Examples of current programs and reruns which meet the above criteria are *The Waltons, The Little House on the Prairie, All in the Family, The Jeffersons, Good Times, The Brady Bunch, Family Feud, Happy Days, Eight Is Enough,* and *One Day at a Time.*)

Step 2: Identify the social or values issue/s raised in the program and formulate it/them into questions or activities. (Many of the value-clarification strategies developed by Simon, *et.al.* can be used effectively to help organize the issue so that students examine alternatives, consequences, patterns of action, and so on. See Chapters 10 and 15 for examples.) For example, having selected an episode from *The Waltons* entitled "The Tempest," the teacher might use a rank-order strategy (see Chapter 10, page 129) to help students explore the values issue, freedom of press. Faced with a situation in which *The Chronicle's* advertisers are cancelling their ads, the Reverend Fordwick and other townsfolk, including Grandma Walton, are upset. Local anti-Nazi activists threaten violence to the Walton family because editor John-Boy Walton has elected to print passages from Hitler's *Mein Kampf* in *The Chronicle.* Should John-Boy have A) stopped printing the passages altogether, B) stuck by his stand and printed them anyway, or C) written a series of articles on how the ignorance and closed-mindedness displayed by many of the townsfolk is more in keeping with Hitler's ideas than with the practice of freedom and democracy?

Step 3: Assign students to watch the selected program.

Step 4: Provide students with a plot summary of the program. This can be in written, and dittoed or xeroxed, or provided by asking students to review what happened.

Step 5: Form students into small groups of (three to five students). Pose the values questions or activities, and ask students to share and compare their responses; or, hold a whole-class discussion by posing the values questions or activities.

Step 6: Ask students to write down several "I learned. . . ." statements about the lesson; then, have them share these with the whole class.

GUIDE 2: PLANNING AND TEACHING A TELEVISION UNIT

Step 1: Select the TV programs to be used as the basis for the unit. Criteria might include the following: Which programs are popular with students? Do students have access to the programs? Which programs raise issues and concepts that are important to study? Are the programs free of violence, sexism, racism, and put-downs?—unless these issues are to be the focus of the unit. (See Guide 1, Step 1 for programs which meet the above criteria.)

Step 2: Identify the issues and/or concepts raised by the programs which are to be examined. Formulate these into questions and/or activities. For example, a unit on television and stereotyping might contain the following questions and activities: What is a stereotype? Are television programs and commercials perpetuating masculine-feminine stereotypes? How is this done? Is television perpetuating minority and ethnic stereotypes? In what ways is television changing the traditional male-female roles? Rewrite an episode which portrays a sexual, racial, or ethnic stereotype so that the program is a more accurate reflection of reality. Interview several children; ask them if women can become doctors, and if men can become nurses. Record their answers. Then ask them if they have ever seen a woman doctor or a male nurse on TV.

Step 3: Develop and assign viewing charts and logs designed to help students focus on the important issues and concepts to be examined. For example, to help students record their observations on television and stereotyping, the chart in Figure 3 might be used.

Figure 3				
Directions: Watch three different programs and the program commercials. Note any instances of stereotypes on the chart below.				
Program-Commercials	Sexual Stereotypes	Racial Stereotypes	Ethnic Stereotypes	Other Stereotypes

Step 4: Form students into small groups and assign the questions and/or activities developed in Step 2. Students are to use their individual viewing-charts and logs to answer and/or do the assigned questions and activities as a group.

Step 5: When the small groups finish, have each group make a report to the whole class. Follow up with class discussions and/or lessons on important topics and concepts.

For more information on developing and using prime-time television lessons in the classroom, as well as membership in PTST, which entitles you to receive monthly mailings during the school year, write:

> PTST (Prime-Time School TV)
> 120 S. LaSalle Street
> Chicago, Ill. 60603

GUIDE 3: IMPLEMENTING THE PHILADELPHIA TV READING PROJECT

Step 1: Provide all students with a copy of the script to be used, and ask them to read a portion of the script by skimming it. (See sample script below.)

Step 2: Using a videotape of the program, have students read along in their scripts with the videotape for five to 12 minutes. (You might think that students will watch the TV videotape rather than read the scripts, but in practice, students tend to read the scripts rather than watch the screen. Occasionally, they look up at the action, but soon return to follow the script.)

Step 3: Develop and teach a mini-lesson based on the reading skills most needed by your students, and which lend themselves most easily to particular treatment in the script. (See sample vocabulary-development lesson below.)

Step 4: Design a practice worksheet of reading-skill exercises developed from the script. Have students do the worksheet in class or assign it as homework.

Step 5: Have students read aloud and act out the portion of the program/script which they have just viewed/read. Assign a student to each of the character parts called for in the script, and assign a student to act as director and read the video directions. By using a video camera and recorder, students can videotape their performance and compare themselves to the stars.

Step 6: Follow up with enrichment activities. Here is where the creative teacher can take tremendous advantage of the captivating nature of television. For example, students can write their own programs. They can write news programs, documentaries on any variety of social issues, historical programs, educational programs like Sesame Street, and serious dramas, as well as the more popular TV fare. By adding a video camera and recorder, students can produce their own programs and make them available to the Instructional Materials Center for use by other classes.

For more details on how to use the Philadelphia Television Reading Project in your school or classroom, write:

> Dr. Bernard Solomon
> Television Reading Program
> Philadelphia Public Schools
> 21st and The Parkway
> Philadelphia, Pa.

On The Horizon

There are really two elements to television—the technical (the hardware) and the programming (the software.) Usually, the technical developments have no significant impact on programming. However, recent developments, such as videotape and the video-cassette technology, permit an entirely different viewpoint to be taken with regard to programming. Currently, a videotape or video-cassette can be played in the classroom or the home, permitting the viewer to stop, instant-replay, or fast-forward as desired. This new use changes the mass-viewing of conventional programs in such a way that specialized programs can now be produced for a limited number of viewers.

Thus, in the near future, you will be able to either purchase, or borrow from a video library, programs such as reading lessons, golf instruction, cooking directions, and so on, in addition to the usual programming that networks mass-feed to television America. With the viewer in charge, television, as we know it, will undergo a revolution. Rather than leaving the viewer passive, this new technology will permit an interactive relationship between the viewer-participant and the television. The addition of cable television, with its potential for two-way communication, will also greatly affect our lifestyles.

Television's impact on society has been enormous. Television's future is yet to be established, as its applications are still to be discovered. Without exaggeration, we can say that the television world will increasingly be the world in which our children will learn, both inside and outside of the classroom.

Sample Script

*The Reading Show**

The Vanishing Shadow, Chapter Nine: "Blazing Bulkheads"

VIDEO DIRECTIONS	SCRIPT
	Gloria: Do you mean that that instrument will counteract the effect of the ray?
	Van Dorn: Not exactly.
FREEZE and slide super:	*Students:* Then this is not an antidote.
Van Dorn picks up a crude version of the vanishing ray.	*Van Dorn:* It will temporarily paralyze the wearer and render him incapable of action. This is the first model of the vanishing ray, charged with the same electrical energy. Take your coat off, slip this on, and I'll demonstate to you.
FREEZE and slide super:	*Students:* You mean demonstrate on you!
Stanley puts on the machine.	*V.O.:* Stanley! Didn't I tell you to look out for that nut??!!
The Professor paralyzes Stanley. Forward and reverse Stanley's jolt, to music.	*Van Dorn:* Now, that's it. Now we take that strap...
	Stanley: Now go easy, Professor. Remember, I'm a friend, not an enemy.
	Van Dorn: I'll remember.
After the dance, FREEZE and slide super:	"TIRED OLD JOKE #4723"
	Gloria: Stop it!
Stanley recovers from the shock.	*Stanley:* If that's the way you treat a friend, heaven help your enemies.

The Reading Show: The Vanishing Shadow, Post-Newsweek Productions, Universal Studios Film; Bernard Soloman and Michael McAndrew creators, co-producers, and writers.

Sample Vocabulary Development Lesson

DIRECTIONS

Following is dialogue taken exactly as it appears in the script. In each sentence, a word is underlined. Find the word or words in the answer box which means the same or nearly the same as the underlined word.

EXAMPLE ONE:

Gloria: Do you mean that that instrument will counteract the effect of the ray?

> **ANSWER BOX**
> 1. neutralize*
> 2. double
> 3. increase

EXAMPLE TWO:

Van Dorn: It will temporarily paralyze the wearer and render him incapable of action.

> **ANSWER BOX**
> 1. permanently
> 2. for a time*
> 3. never

EXAMPLE THREE:

Van Dorn: This is the first model of the vanishing ray, charged with the same electrical energy. Take your coat off, slip this on, and I'll demonstrate to you.

> **ANSWER BOX**
> 1. ruin
> 2. completely destroy
> 3. explain by using examples*

*Correct answer

13 HOW TO USE TV AS A CREATIVE BABYSITTER WITHOUT FEELING GUILTY

HOW TO USE TV
AS A CREATIVE
BABYSITTER
WITHOUT FEELING
GUILTY

Researchers estimate that our children watch an average of 54 hours of television each week.[1] This is primarily due to the fact that many parents, being busy and over-extended people, use television to "electronically babysit" their children. Of course, 54 hours a week of television is not good for children. Children also need plenty of physical play, to develop their motor skills and coordination; of creative play, to develop their imagination and creativity; and of social play, to develop their social interaction skills, moral reasoning abilities, and thinking skills. Most parents are aware of this, at least intuitively, and thus feel guilty about the amount of television their children view. In a very real sense, parents face a difficult dilemma; they know that too much television is not good for their children, but they feel pressured to get their own work finished, and television is such a convenient babysitter.

One way out of the dilemma is to use TV as a "creative babysitter." Many television programs can be used as a stimulus for further play. Having watched a half-hour or hour TV show, children can then be encouraged to play for an hour or two on their own, recreating and acting out their own version of the show they have just viewed.

For example, after the children have watched *Land of the Lost,* suggest that they pretend that they are lost in an unknown land. Help them recreate the appropriate environment by suggesting that the dining-room table, covered with a blanket, has become the home cave, a bedroom closet has become the sleez-stick cave, and so on. Each child can be a different character from the TV show, and act out their own version of the most recent episode. Help them find hand-props to use as equipment.

I suggest using the following guidelines to get the most physical, creative, and social play for your children, and time for you.

1. Allow children to view a television program (30 minutes or one hour in length).

2. Brainstorm with your children ways that they could recreate and act out their own version of the show. Help them think about what rooms, materials, furniture, etc., can be used to recreate the environment; what props can be used to simulate the equipment and vehicles used on the show; what characters they would like to play, and so on (5 to 15 minutes).

3. Children, then, on their own, or with a little help from you, are to recreate the environment and props in as simple or as elaborate a way as you and they desire. This might involve setting up chairs in a row to serve as a train or bus; putting a sheet over a table

to serve as a tent or house; or using building blocks to simulate the outlines of buildings, spaceships, streets, and so on (5 to 30 minutes).

4. Once the environment is recreated, children can then recreate and act out their own version of the program. You might help them get started by playing with them for five minutes or so. Young children, especially, appreciate your help, because it helps to show them how to play "let's pretend" (30 minutes to two hours.)

5. Clean up. Everything gets put back where it belongs (5 to 15 minutes).

Footnote

[1]Mankiewicz, Frank, and Joel Swerdlow, *Remote Control*, Times Books, New York, 1978.

PART III

HOW TO PREPARE YOUR CHILD TO LIVE IN A TV WORLD

14 INTRODUCTION TO PART III

After an exhaustive study of television's impact upon our society, the authors of *Remote Control* conclude that, "Nearly every aspect of American life is now shaped, in one way or another, by television." Voting behavior is influenced by the candidates use of TV. Family relationships are changed by both the role-depiction of TV characters and the amount of time families spend watching TV (often on separate sets). The sale of products, as well as dietary preferences and values, are largely determined by the companies that can afford to buy the network commercials. Attitudes and beliefs about such things as the safeness of our communities come from fictional crime-programs, rather than from reality-based information sources such as newspapers or personal experience. Even the U.S. Constitution may be being altered as a result of police shows depicting law-enforcement agents flagrantly violating individual civil rights as protected under the Fourth, Fifth, and Sixth Amendments. Two studies suggest that TV has served to "soften public opinion," and to allow Supreme Court decisions which have legalized such police conduct. Without question, television is the most powerful force shaping our world today.

As we noted earlier, most of television's powerful impact, especially upon our children, is negative. This need not be so, but it is the reality of present television programming. As a result, we parents, and anyone who works with or teaches children, must take steps to prepare children to live in a television-dominated world, so that they are not negatively affected by the worst on television, and can cope intelligently and effectively with the changes TV is producing in our culture and social institutions. For one thing, schools and colleges should begin offering required courses on the effects of television on our lives; parents should be encouraged to read books like *Remote Control* and *The Plug-In Drug*, and then discuss them with their children; newspapers and magazines should begin doing features and editorials on the effects of television; television itself should produce documentaries on its own impact; more money should be poured into investigating and researching the effects of television, and these new findings should be widely distributed. Parents and community-service groups should organize and put pressure on the TV networks and sponsors to improve the quality of television programming and reduce or eliminate misleading and fraudulent television advertising. Parents and community-service groups should organize and put pressure on government officials to provide and enforce stronger standards for improved television programming and advertising. And most important, parents and teachers must help children to 1) learn to make sound value judgments and decisions about what they view on TV, and 2) develop the self-confidence and self-esteem to stand up against the subtle but strong pressures exerted by television programming and commercials. If these things were

Box 3

Television advertising can serve a very real and useful purpose in our society, when it informs people about the availability of various goods and services. This is helpful information. However, all too often, TV ads go beyond this, and try to sell us a product that the sponsor overtly or covertly claims will give us more sex-appeal, help us make friends, give us more prestige, and so on. Now, when we sit down and think about XYZ brand of toothpaste giving us more sex-appeal—as the ad suggests by showing us a woman overcome with passion after the man brushes his teeth with XYZ brand—it is just plain nonsense, and irrational. It is so ludicrous and irrational, that we just smile at it, and perhaps think, how corny! These ads can, however, have a very powerful subliminal effect upon us, especially if we have a poor self-concept in the area at which the ad is directed.

For example, let's say that a teenage boy doesn't feel that he is very attractive to others, and thus is very needy in this area. He very much, perhaps even desperately, wants to be given affection by the opposite sex. Now, we know that such a needy person is not going to think as rationally as a person whose self-esteem in regard to the opposite sex is high. So, along comes this moronic little ad about XYZ toothpaste, and *wham*, our teenage boy in need of affection buys it. "Maybe it will work," his subconscious mind says, and so he goes out and buys and uses XYZ religiously. To say the least, this kind of advertising is a rip-off; it is aimed at people's feelings of inadequacy, and tries to sell them a bill of goods which in reality won't make them feel any more adequate at all.

Children and adolescents with low feelings of self-esteem are also very vulnerable and susceptible to believing everything they see on TV, from political propaganda, to sex and race stereotypes, to highly-fictionalized and often fantasy-oriented accounts of how such people as doctors, lawyers, and policemen operate. The pattern is pernicious, and only parental vigilance and challenges can counteract this cheap-shot brainwashing.

done, we might then begin to see television as a powerful positive force in our children's development.

However, we need not sit around and wait for all of the above to happen. Unfortunately, if we did, we would probably sit around for a long time to come. We can, as parents and teachers, begin to prepare our children to live in a TV world. The two chapters included in this third part of the book can help in that preparation. The activities in Chapter 15, "Family Time," can help your children develop the valuing skills they need to make sound judgments and decisions about what they see on TV. The activities in Chapter 16, "Special Time," can help your children develop the self-esteem they need to stand up to the pressure exerted on them by television programs and commercials. (For an example of how television can influence a person with low self-esteem, see Box 3.)

15 FAMILY TIME: VALUE CLARIFICATION ACTIVITIES TO PREPARE YOUR CHILD FOR A TV WORLD

FAMILY TIME: VALUE CLARIFICATION ACTIVITIES TO PREPARE YOUR CHILD FOR A TV WORLD

"Family Time" is the name we have given to the time each day when the whole family does something together. Family time might be spent playing a game in the evening, going on a Sunday picnic, or doing many of the conventional "family things" together. However, we also use family time to do some special activities included in this chapter. The aim of these activities is to help our children develop the valuing skills they need to make sound choices and decisions about the things they encounter on TV, in school, and with their peers.* Family time can also help to improve and strengthen family relationships and communication.

To use these activities in the family setting, simply follow the instructions provided. To use them in the

*For a rationale and theory behind the valuing activities in this chapter, see Chapter 10: "How To Use TV To Nurture Your Child's Value and Moral Development."

classroom or church-school setting, simply substitute teacher for parent, and students for children.

WHOBODY LIKES . . . . (FAMILY VALUES-VOTING TIME)

Purpose

When my daughter was two years old, my wife and I began doing values-clarification activities at the dinner table. One of our favorite activities was values voting. Values voting serves as a quick and simple way to start children thinking about and taking a public stand on values issues. Initially, we would ask questions like, "Who likes to ride on trains?" or, "Who likes ice cream?" Then, we would put our thumbs up to answer "yes" and put our thumbs down to answer "no." Our daughter really enjoyed playing the voting games. Within a short period, she started asking voting questions. However, she started her questions with the phrase, "Whobody likes. . . ." to begin our family values-voting time.

Instructions

To do values voting with your family, select several of the questions below, or make up your own questions. Pose the questions and ask those who agree to put their thumbs up (both thumbs if they strongly agree), and those who disagree to put their thumbs down (both thumbs down to strongly disagree). Encourage family members to give the reasons for the way they voted.

The following is a list of sample values-voting questions:

1. Who likes asparagus?

2. Who would like to be famous someday?

3. Who would like to change the color of your hair, just for fun?

4. Who would like to have more children in our family?

5. Who thinks school is an exciting place?

6. Who thinks older children should be allowed to discipline younger children?

7. Who likes to spend most of your free time watching TV?

8. Who likes to spend your time outside whenever possible?

9. Who would enjoy making Christmas presents this year?

10. Who thinks it is OK for men to wear wigs?

11. Who would turn your best friend into the police for using drugs? For pushing drugs?

12. Who thinks school attendance should be completely voluntary?

13. Who had a good day today? Who had a bad day today?

14. Who would like to take a trip to the moon someday?

15. Who would like to learn how to sail? Ski?

16. Who would like to learn to play a musical instrument?

17. Who likes to go for walks in the woods?

18. Who would like to be a U.S. senator or president someday?

19. Who thinks we should wear seatbelts whenever riding in a car?

20. Who would prefer to live in the country? In the city?

21. Who would enjoy having someone famous for a friend?

22. Who feels that cheating is sometimes justified?

23. Who enjoys going on family picnics?

24. Who is in love right now?

25. Who thinks children should work for their allowances?

26. Who would be in favor of spending the family vacation camping this year?

27. Who thinks it's OK for boys to play with dolls?

28. Who has read a book just for fun in the past month?

29. Who thinks it is OK to tell a white lie to save a friend's reputation?

30. Who thinks it is difficult to be happy without money?

FAMILY CIRCLE TIME

Purpose

Family Circle Time is a very special time each week. Family members pull their chairs into a circle, or sit on the floor in a circle. A special topic is selected, and each family member gets a turn to talk about the topic while the others listen. Family members listen in a very special way. Instead of hearing part of what the focus person says, and then thinking their own thoughts about it, family members try to hear *everything* the focus person says and feels, without evaluating it. When this happens, family members begin to trust each other more, and to share the things that really concern them, things that they probably would not share except with their most trusted friends.

Just ask yourself how many times your children get five minutes of your undivided attention. For that matter, how many times do *you* get five minutes of anybody's undivided attention? Not many times is my guess, and yet, giving five minutes to each family member, and to ourselves, is one of the most important things we can do to nurture our children's and our own personal growth.

Instructions

To hold Family Circle Time, set aside a time each week on a regular basis. Select a topic of discussion from the list below, or make up your own topics. Introduce the procedures and rules which follow, and follow them.

Procedures

1. Each family member gets a turn to be the focus person and talk about the topic.

2. Each person gets listened to and gets feedback when he or she is the focus person.

Rules

1.   The rule of focusing

The focus person can talk as much or as little about the selected topic as he or she wishes. Other family members are to give the focus person their full, undivided attention. It is not the non-focus person's place to agree, interrupt, disagree or ask questions. Such behavior violates the rule of focusing.

2.   The rule of acceptance

Each person attempts to communicate acceptance to the focus person. This does not mean that each person must agree with the focus person; rather, it means that each person agrees to accept the right of the focus person to say what he or she thinks and feels is true. Acceptance is communicated by smiling, nodding, leaning closer, saying "yes" or "uh-huh," and maintaining eye contact. Nonacceptance is communicated by frowning, shaking your head, pulling away, drumming your fingers, looking at your watch, stony silence, or refusing to make or maintain eye contact.

3. The rule of reflective listening

After the focus person has finished talking, a family member volunteers to reflect or feed back to the focus person the essence of what he or she talked about, and how he/she felt about what the focus person talked about. Others in the group should be encouraged to help the volunteer recall the points made by the focus person, as well as the feelings he/she was expressing.

A nice way to end Family Circle Time is to have one or two members (or the whole family) try to recall and summarize the points made by each person when he or she was the focus person.

A List of Family Circle Topics

1. A time I felt really good.

2. A time I felt really bad.

3. A time I felt angry.

4. A time I felt sad.

5. I did something that helped someone feel good.

6. I did something that made me feel both good and bad.

7. A time I felt disgusted.

8. A time I felt hurt.

9. A time I felt like getting even.

10. Somebody did something, and I felt resentful.

11. A time I really loved someone.

12. A time I really hated someone.

13. A time I felt very depressed.

14. How I feel when I win at something.

15. How I feel when I lose at something.

16. A time I felt proud.

17. A time I felt afraid.

18. A time I felt embarrassed.

19. A time I felt very bored.

20. A time I felt like crying but didn't.

21. Somebody did something about which I felt both good and bad.

22. Something that I feel very joyful about.

23. A time I felt happy.

24. A time I had very mixed feelings about something.

25. Something I am proud of about my family.

26. What I look for in choosing a friend.

27. A difficult choice I have had to make.

28. A belief or value I feel very strongly about.

29. A stand I have taken that took courage.

30. Something I have done that I would now do differently.

31. A change I would like to make in myself.

32. My favorite place.

33. If I could have three wishes, what they would be.

34. A choice I made that turned out well.

35. A choice I made that did not turn out well.

36. A choice that I made that others thought was wrong, but I made the choice anyway.

37. What I would do if I had only one year to live.

38. Something I did that took courage.

FAMILY INTERVIEW TIME

Purpose

The Family Interview gives each family member a chance to be interviewed by the other family members. It is an opportunity for each family member to have the spotlight for a short period of time, to discuss and explain his or her views on a variety of subjects and topics. During the process, a good deal of values-related thinking occurs.

Instructions

To hold a Family Interview, choose a time

when the whole family is together; e.g., just after dinner, Sunday afternoon, or whenever. One member of the family volunteers to be interviewed. Conduct the interview by using the following rules:

1. The interviewee may pass on any question, by simply saying, "I pass."

2. The interviewee may end the interview at any time, by simply saying, "Thank you for the interview."

3. The interviewee may ask the interviewer any of the questions asked of him or her after the interview is over.

Here are some sample interview questions:

1. Where would you like to spend the family vacation this year?

2. What is something you would really like to learn to do?

3. What is your favorite TV show? Movie? Place?

4. What do you like best about school? Least?

5. Who are two people, not including family, whom you really admire?

6. If you could change something about the world we live in, what would you change?

7. What do you see yourself doing five years from now? What would you like to be doing then?

8. What is the most important book you have read recently? Why?

9. If you could change something about yourself, what would it be?

10. What is your most prized possession?

11. What do you enjoy most in life?

12. What would have to happen to make you feel like leaving our country?

13. If you could be any age, what age would you choose to be? Why?

14. What do you look for in choosing a friend?

15. If you could live any place in the world for one year, where would it be?

16. If someone gave you a gift of $100, what would you do with it?

17. Do you think you will make a good husband/wife? Father/mother?

18. What do you see as the most important turning point(s) in your life?

19. What do you think you want to do with your life?

20. If you had only one year to live, what would you like to do in that year?

A FAMILY AUCTION

Purpose

This is an enjoyable game, which can raise a host of values issues and provide a great deal of discussion among family members. The idea is to conduct a family auction, in which family members bid for certain items by placing their bids in a sealed envelope. Because each member is given a specified amount of points or play-money to bid with, he or she must set priorities and bid on those items which are most wanted.

Instructions

To conduct the auction, provide each family member with a set amount of play-money, points, or chips; let's say, 1,000 points or play-dollars. Then, use the auction list below, or make up a list that is more appropriate to your family, and let each member think about the list privately. Next, each member writes down which items he or she wants to bid on, and puts down how much he or she wants to bid beside each item. The total bid must not exceed the amount allocated to each person. Then the bids are placed in a sealed envelope. Finally, at some appropriate time when the whole family is together, the sealed bids are opened. Whoever has the highest bid for an item "wins" that item. The aim is, of course, not to win but to generate discussion between family members about why each wants certain items more than others.

Sample Auction Items:

1. You become a famous movie star.

2. You receive an appointment as ambassador to the country of your choice.

3. You win an all-expense-paid trip to Disney World for two weeks.

4. You have a photographic memory.

5. For one year, you get to shop for clothes free.

6. The boy or girl friend of your choice becomes your beau.

7. You get elected to the U.S. Senate.

8. You are chosen to receive the Outstanding Man/Woman of the Year Award.

9. You discover how to cure and prevent cancer.

10. You win the Nobel Peace Prize for stopping war for the next 50 years.

11. You will have good health for the next 25 years.

12. You acquire several hundred feet of ocean-front property.

13. You become the number-one expert in the field of your choice.

14. You receive a small family inheritance, which provides you with financial security for life.

15. You get to do whatever you want, wherever you want, for the next five years.

A FAMILY COAT OF ARMS

Purpose

This activity helps family members think about what they are doing as a family. It helps to build a feeling of family unity, and serves to give the family unit a purposeful direction.

Instructions

Have someone in the family draw a shield (See the figure below). Then, family members are to discuss and agree upon a picture or symbol to place in each of the sections of the shield. Family members can take turns drawing the pictures or symbols on the shield.

1. In the upper left-hand corner, draw a picture of the family's greatest achievement or success.

2. In the upper right-hand corner, draw a picture of the family's greatest strength.

3. In the lower left-hand corner, draw a picture of the family's dream or goal.

4. In the lower right-hand corner, draw a picture of a value that the entire family holds dear.

5. In the banner under the shield, write three words or a motto that best describes the essence or image of the family.

Then display the shield in the family room, or in some other appropriate place in the home. You might want to draw the shield on a large sheet of posterboard, using poster paints or magic markers.

Here are some additional items that can be used on the shield:

1. Draw a picture of something the family enjoys doing together.

2. Draw a picture of the family's greatest adventure together.

3. Draw a picture of each family member's outstanding characteristic, ability, contribution, etc.

"DEAR ABBY" TIME

Purpose

This activity helps children learn to solve personal problems in a thoughtful and systematic manner. It also gives each family member a chance to share his or her viewpoint on various important value and moral issues.

Instructions

Select a "Dear Abby" or other lonelyhearts letter, such letters appear in most major newspapers—and read the letter to the whole family. Encourage each family member to play "Abby," and to respond to the letter with his or her advice. Then, read "Abby's" advice aloud. Compare notes. Examine the possible consequences of each point of view. Help your children to think of other alternatives to propose, and examine these alternatives.

As a follow-up, you might suggest that the family start a "Dear Abby" bulletin board. Family members can write "Dear Abby" letters concerning their own problems or questions, and post these letters on the bulletin board. Family members can take turns being "Abby," and answer the letters. Or, the "Dear Abby" letters can be discussed at a family meeting.

VALUES DILEMMAS FOR THE FAMILY

Purpose

This activity gives children practice in solving values problems, by carefully thinking through various alternative courses of action and weighing the consequences of each.

Instructions

Select one of the values problems below, and pose it to your family. Then, have family members discuss the following questions:

1. What decision would you make, and/or action would you take, concerning this values problem?

2. What might be some of the possible consequences both pro and con making this decision or taking this action? How would you be affected? Who else might be affected? How would they be affected?

3. Can you think of any alternative ways to handle or solve this problem? What are they? What might be the consequences and outcomes of these alternatives?

4. How do you feel about your decision? Do you feel good about it? Do you have misgivings?

5. Have you ever found yourself in a situation similar to this? What did you do? What were the consequences and results?

Broken Promise

Billy promised his father that he wouldn't climb trees any more after the boy next door was hurt very badly when he fell out of a tree. On the way home from school, Billy sees a kitten in the lower branches of a tree. The kitten is very frightened. It would be easy for Billy to get the kitten down. What should Billy do: break his promise to his father, or leave the frightened kitten in the tree?

Finders Keepers

Eddie and Mary are playing hide-and-go-seek in the park. Eddie discovers a billfold with $5.00 in it. There are no identification cards in the billfold. Eddie wants to keep the $5.00 and put it toward a family bicycle, which he and Mary have been saving for. Mary thinks they should give the billfold and the $5.00 to the park guard, in case someone comes back looking for it. What do you think Eddie and Mary should do?

Baseball or a Surprise Party?

Bobby's classmates have decided to throw a surprise

going-away party, since Bobby is going to live with his father in another state in August. Bobby's best friend tells him about the surprise party, but swears Bobby to secrecy. On Monday, Bobby's father phones his mother to tell her that he plans to take Bobby and his brother to a major-league baseball game on Friday afternoon. Friday is the day of the surprise party. Bobby would prefer to go to the baseball game with his father, since he enjoys baseball and also doesn't get to see his father very often. He knows that his classmates will be disappointed. He could easily say that he didn't know about the surprise party. What should he do?

Telling Tales

Ted brags to his friend John that he knows how to get into the school when it is locked. The next day, the principal reports that the school has been broken into and vandalized. What should John do?

To Pull or Not to Pull the Plug

Ann, age 19, goes into a coma after taking drugs and alcohol. She has been in a coma for several months, and is being kept alive with the help of an artificial respirator. Doctors say that there is no hope that Ann will recover, because of severe brain damage. A court decision has recently been made which will allow Ann's parents to instruct the doctors to pull the plug and let her die. What should they do?

Ecology vs Unemployment

Jim and Mary have been married for several years. Jim is president of his own large corporation, and Mary has just been appointed Director of Environmental Protection for the region. Mary learns that Jim's company is pouring hazardous pollutants into the air at night. She also knows that if Jim's company is forced to clean up its chimneys, the cost could force the company to close, which could produce financial disaster for the local community. What should Mary do?

FAMILY DISCUSSION TIME

Purpose

Family discussions can be highly entertaining as well as instructive, especially if debate focuses on important value and social issues. Some of the most important learning I did as an adolescent happened as a result of family discussions in which each person *felt free* to express his or her own point of view. I often went into these discussions with one point of view, and after listening to others' points of view, emerged from the discussion with a new point of view. The key to successful family discussions is that each person must *feel free* to express his or her own point of view.

Instructions

To hold a family discussion, appoint a time, such as dinner or an evening by the fire. Select a question from one of the categories below, and pose the question to the entire family. Each person should have time to express his or her point of view.

If you are leading a family discussion, you can help

family members feel free to express themselves by following these guidelines:

1. Insist that family members respect each other's right to express themselves without being laughed at, ridiculed, called "stupid" or put down in some other way.

2. If you disagree with someone (especially your children) don't moralize, preach, or threaten to teach them a lesson. Rather, simply say that you disagree with their view and give your reasons. Then let them decide. It will be much more effective than trying to force them to change. And remember, they could be right.

Family
• What do you think is the biggest problem in families today? What can be done about it?

• Should a family take at least one week long vacation a year together?

• Should teenage children be expected to pay some or all of their board and room expenses at home?

Friends
• Should you tell a friend that he or she has bad breath? Body odor?

• Would you leave a party where people were using illegal drugs, even though your best friend refused to leave with you?

• Is it better to have a few friends or many friends?

• Would you let a friend copy from your work if he or she didn't have his/her work finished?

Environment
• Should the development of atomic power plants be banned in the U.S.?
• Should the federal government subsidize waste recycling plants?
• Which is more important, economic progress or the environment?

Health
• Should smoking be banned in all public places?
• Should food additives be prohibited?

Leisure Time
• Should children be allowed to watch as much TV as they want?
• Is it important to have a hobby?
• Is television helpful or harmful to society?

Love and Sex
• Is it OK for a ten-year-old to go steady?
• Is it OK to have sexual relations before marriage?
• Should homosexuals be allowed to hold public jobs?
• Would you be in favor of one-year trial marriages?
• Should an unwed, pregnant girl be encouraged to get an abortion?
• Is it OK for a couple to use artificial insemination

when the husband is sterile?

- Should junior-high age children be given full birth control information?
- Is sex without love wrong or immoral?
- Would you be in favor of abortions on demand?
- Is our society becoming too sexually permissive?

Marriage and Divorce
- Should people wait as long as possible to marry?
- Would you be in favor of contract marriages which must be renewed every two years?
- Is it ok for an unwed mother or father to raise children alone?
- Would you object to your son or daughter living with someone who has no intention of getting married?
- Is it important to get engaged before getting married?
- Should the consent of both marriage partners be the only legal grounds for getting a divorce?
- Should divorce be made illegal?
- Should couples know each other a certain length of time before getting married?
- Is taking a honeymoon important?

Money
- Is it important to give money to charities?
- Is it important to regularly save money in a savings account?

- Is merit-pay a good thing?
- Could you work at a job you hated if it paid enough?
- Does well-known brand-name merchandise give you more for your money than less well-known brand name merchandise?
- Is it important to be wealthy?
- Should the wealth in this country be redistributed?
- Should older children be paid for babysitting for younger brothers and sisters?

Moral Judgments
- Are there times when cheating is justified?
- Is honesty always the best policy?
- Should looking out for number one be your first concern?

Personal Tastes
- Should children be allowed to pick out and choose their own clothes?
- Is it OK for men to wear wigs or hair pieces?
- Should children be allowed to wear their hair in any style they choose?

Politics
- Will writing to your congressman or to the president do any good?
- Should the voting age be lowered in the U.S.?
- Is our political system bringing justice and equal opportunity to all?

- Is democracy dying in the world?
- Should a person who advocates the overthrow of democracy be allowed to run for political office?
- Should all people in the world have the same rights and freedoms?

Race
- Should everyone have at least one friend of another race? If you don't associate with members of other races, does that mean you are prejudiced?
- Are inter-racial marriages a good thing? Would you object if your child wants to marry someone of another race?

Religion
- Is it important that people attend religious services regularly?
- Should children be made to go to religious services even if they don't want to go?
- Has organized religion outlived its usefulness in this day and age?
- Is there life after death?
- Is our destiny mostly determined by luck, or by God, or by ourselves?
- Should you embrace your parents' faith, or choose a religion for yourself?
- Is there such a thing as absolute good and absolute evil?

Rules, Regulations, and Laws
- What is the right age for parents to allow their kids to go to drive-in movies?
- Is capital punishment a good idea?
- Should our society have teenage correctional institutions?
- Should hitchhiking be outlawed?
- Should sexual mores be legislated?
- Should men and women be equal before the law in all respects?

Safety
- Is it important for people to wear seatbelts when traveling?
- Should we have a national speed-limit in the U.S.?

School
- Should school attendance be completely voluntary at all ages?
- Should students pay for their own schooling?
- Do letter-grades and report cards help motivate students to learn?
- Should sex-education be included in the school curriculum?
- Is competition in school important to prepare students for the real world?
- Do schools do a good job of preparing students for college? For careers? For life?

- Should schools teach right and wrong values?
- Is a voucher plan to allow students to attend any school of their (and their parents') choice a good idea?
- Should testing and grading be abolished in public schools?
- Should teachers be allowed to paddle or hit students who misbehave?
- Do students have too much freedom in schools today?

Welfare
- Should welfare programs for the poor be drastically reduced?
- Should there be minimum guaranteed wages?

Women's Rights/Roles
- Should mothers devote their full attention to raising their children?
- Should men take an equal role in cleaning, cooking, and other household duties?
- Are there alternatives to the nuclear family, for raising children?
- Should fathers share equally in the task of raising children?
- Should the Equal Rights Amendment to the Constitution be passed?
- Should a quota system be established for hiring women?

- Is our present form of marriage outmoded?

TAKING INVENTORY

Purpose

This activity helps family members reflect on how they have acted on their values in the past, and how they intend to act on them in the future.

Instructions

Select several of the questions below, and pose them to your family. Each person gets a chance to answer each question. Then compare notes.

1. Have you ever written a letter to the editor?

2. Do you consider yourself a leader?

3. Will you use natural childbirth to deliver your child?

4. Will you ever run for public office?

5. Will you retire at age 50?

6. Do you have a savings account which you use regularly?

7. Have you ever changed the color of your hair?

8. Do you consider yourself a civil-rights advocate?

9. Do you belong to a book club?

10. Have you ever considered changing your religion?

11. Have you ever cheated on a test?

12. Do you lock all the windows and doors and pull down the shades when you are in the house alone?

13. Do you wear a seatbelt when traveling in an automobile?

14. Will you be a good mother/father someday?

15. Will you need a lot of money to be happy?

16. Have you ever wished you could be famous?

17. Will you raise your children less strictly than you were raised?

18. Do you consider yourself a TV nut?

19. Have you ever told someone that he or she has bad breath?

20. Do you enjoy attending religious services?

21. Do you have a good friend of another religion? Of another race? Of another sex?

22. Will you belong to the same political party as your parents?

23. Do you think about death often?

24. Have you ever been camping out-of-doors?

25. Will you give your body to medical science when you die?

26. Have you ever given money to a charity?

27. Do you buy and use only well-known brand-name merchandise?

28. Will you have your body cremated when you die?

29. Have you ever been friendly to someone you couldn't stand?

30. Do you have more than five pairs of shoes?

31. Do you pick up hitchhikers?

32. Will you go to college?

33. Do you enjoy traveling?

34. Will you be involved in a sport (e.g., playing tennis, golf, etc.) when you are 45?

35. Will you choose a career which will give you security?

FAMILY GUESTS

Purpose

This activity helps family members explore their own and each other's values priorities as these are reflected in the persons they would invite to a dinner party.

Instructions

Pose the following problem to your family: "Imagine that you can invite anyone to dinner at our house, and he or she will come; the invited guest can be living or dead, famous or infamous, rich or poor. Whom would you like to invite?"

Have each family member make a guest list of five persons. When the lists are complete, have each person share his or her list of guests and the reasons why each was invited. What characteristics do each of the invited guests that are valued possess?

As an optional follow-up activity, have family members come to a consensus on a list of seven guests to be invited.

OUR FAVORITE THINGS

Purpose
This activity is a good way to help children examine what things are really important to them.

Instructions
Pose this problem to your family: "What if there were a fire in our house, and we only had a few minutes to gather up a few of our most prized possessions? What would we want to save?"

Have each family member make a list of all his or her favorite things, including clothes, play-things, sports equipment, musical equipment, keepsakes, family heirlooms, etc. Then, each person is to put the number one beside the item he or she would most want to save, a two beside the second item he or she would next like to save, and so on, until the whole list is ranked.

Then, family members take turns sharing their rank-ordered lists.

VALUES STEMS

Purpose

This is a good activity to use on family trips. It can also be used at the dinner table, at family get-togethers, or on an individual basis with your children. It helps children reflect on personal and value issues.

Instructions

Have each family member complete a sentence stem. This can be done in writing or verbally. Each family member then gets a turn to share his completed sentence, and elaborate upon it if he or she wishes.

Here are some sample sentence stems:

1. If I could be. . . .

2. I wish Mom/Dad would. . . .

3. If I could change my age I. . . .

4. Our family. . . .

5. The thing I like best about our family is. . . .

6. When I'm a Mom/Dad. . . .

7. Sometimes I wish. . . .

8. When I grow up. . . .

9. I'm most happy when. . . .

10. Sometimes I'm afraid of. . . .

11. People make me sad when. . . .

12. One thing I don't like. . . .

13. I hope someday I/we. . . .

14. One of my favorite times was. . . .

15. I hope my family. . . .

16. I hope my children won't have to. . . .

17. My brother(s)/sister(s). . . .

FAMILY VALIDATIONS

Purpose

This activity helps family members learn to validate and appreciate each other.

Instructions

On a regular basis, each day, or at the end of the week, set aside 15 or 20 minutes for family validations; I suggest doing this at the dinner table, or when the whole family is together. Each person has his or her turn to appreciate something he or she has done, and to be appreciated by the others.

Appreciations are very difficult for some of us to hear, especially self-appreciations. Underneath, we really love and want appreciation, but we have learned, via our culture, that bragging and boasting about ourselves is wrong, and that modesty is good. Thus, we have often been punished for showing pride, and have been rewarded for deprecating ourselves. The problem is that this self-deprecating part of us usually turns into a real "vulture," which eats away at our feelings of self-confidence. Thus, you may have to remind your children to cage their vultures in this activity. You will probably hear the vulture a lot. The vulture is tearing away when children use such phrases as:

"I'm kind-of good at. . . ."

"I was pretty good at. . . ."

"I wasn't too bad at. . . ."

"All in all, I. . . ."

"Relatively speaking, I. . . ."

These phrases qualify the experience, and, in effect, negate a portion of the experience. Encourage children to come right out and own up to their positive feelings, without qualifying them. Watch out for children who can not look at their strengths without also pointing out their weaknesses; this too, is the vulture tearing away.

FAMILY SECRET PAL

Purpose

This is an enjoyable way to foster and demonstrate caring in the family. This activity helps to build good feelings and family unity.

Instructions

Place each family member's name on a slip of

paper, and put the folded slips in a hat. Each person draws the name of his family secret pal. Secret pals are to do nice things for their pals without giving themselves away. For example, a secret pal might send his or her pal a card or a small home-made gift. Or, the secret pal might do the dishes, wash the car, clean up a bedroom or do some other chore when the secret pal's beneficiary isn't around. Family members can remain secret pals for a day, a week, a month, or a year, depending upon the age of the children and family preference. At some point, the secret pals reveal their identity.

THE FAMILY MAILBOX

Purpose

The family mailbox is a great way for you to let your children know that you appreciate them. They will love and cherish the letters they get from you, even if the letters are only a sentence long, or consist of three little words, like, "I love you."

Instructions

Help your children make a family mailbox. Any small box with a cover and a slit in the top, large enough to put a letter in, will do. Or, if your children prefer, each family member can have his or her own mailbox. The family mailbox(es) can be decorated or left plain. Tell your children that the family mailbox-(es) will provide another way that family members can communicate with each other, even though their days are busy and fully scheduled. Whenever someone in the family wants to say something to someone else, one way he/she can do this is to write the person a letter or short note, and put the communciation in the family mailbox. At the end of each day or week, the mailbox will be opened and the letters delivered to the person to whom they are addressed.

Leave a note pad, some envelopes, and a pencil near the family mailbox, so that children do not have to hunt for pencil and paper every time they want to write a letter and use the family mailbox.

Provide your children with some guidelines as to what might be put in the letters. For example, they might wish to write a thank-you letter for something that a family member has done for them. Or, they might write a letter telling another family member how much they appreciate them in some way. Or, they might write a letter sharing some personal problem. The family mailbox, however, is not a place to write letters which criticize or put another family member down. Nor is it a place for anonymous letters.

DINNER TABLE REFLECTIONS

Purpose

This activity helps children think about what they have done or learned each day that is worthwhile. If your children have not been doing or learning worthwhile things, it won't take many reflections before they

they begin to think of worthwhile things to share with the family.

Instructions

At each evening meal, when the whole family is together, ask each person to share something of what he/she has done or learned that day that is worthwhile. It may be something learned or relearned; something done for someone else; something thought about or discovered; something accomplished, or so forth. Sometimes, the following sentence stems can be helpful in getting children started.

I learned that. . . .

I relearned that. . . .

I discovered that. . . .

I helped someone to. . . .

Something I accomplished is. . . .

I thought a lot about. . . .

Mom and Dad should share what they have done that was worthwhile, too!

VALIDATION SCAVENGER HUNT

Purpose

This is a great activity to do while picnicking at a park. It helps family members appreciate one another, and builds self-esteem.

Instructions

Have each family member choose a partner—Mom and Dad should play, too. If there are uneven numbers, put everyone in a circle. Tell them, "The person on your right is going to be the person for whom you are going to go on a Validation Scavenger Hunt. For the next 15 or 20 minutes each of you is to go looking for three things that represent for you this person's three greatest strengths or assets. You may go in pairs or trios, but not with your partner. Here are some examples of what you might look for. For John, I might find 1) a stone which represents his great strength and endurance, 2) an inch-worm which represents his extreme patience and persistence in taking one step at a time to achieve his goal, and 3) a long branch to represent his willingness to reach out to others when they need help.

When everyone returns from the scavenger hunt, have each person share what they have found, and what it represents, with the whole family. This sharing is bound to be the highlight of the picnic.

CHILDREN'S DAY

Purpose

Mom and Dad each have their special day, so why shouldn't children in the family also have their special day? A special day is a way to let children know that they are appreciated.

Instructions

Let your children choose a Sunday when nothing else will interfere to be their special day. On that Sunday, your children get to do whatever they want. They do not have to do chores or run errands. They can order whatever they want (within reason, of course) for breakfast, lunch, and dinner. This Sunday is Children's Day. Mom and Dad might even make a special Children's Day card to give their offspring, or buy them special Children's Day gifts.

As a variation, each child might have a special day devoted entirely to himself or herself. The child's birthday could serve as an occasion not merely for gift-giving, but for special activities oriented around the birthday child.

DEAD-LETTER BOX[1]

Purpose

What does your family do with its negative feelings? If your family is like most families, far too often, negative feelings either get pent up until they explode in a battle, or are communicated in a very destructive way. The Dead-Letter Box is one effective way to help family members express their anger and aggressive feelings without doing damage to each other's "I-am-lovable-and-capable" feelings.

Instructions

Find a small box—an old shoe box works perfectly—and cut a slit in the cover, just large enough so that envelopes can be inserted. Then, tape the cover shut with masking tape, and write on the outside of the box, Dead-Letter Box. Tell family members that from now on, instead of keeping those hateful and hurtful feelings pent up or venting them verbally to each other, they are to write their splenetic emotions on a slip of paper, enclose the paper in an envelope, and put it in the Dead-Letter Box. At the end of the week (or when the box is full), the whole family meets, opens the box, and burns or destroys the letters without looking at them. The no-peeking rule is to be *strictly* enforced.

You will find the Dead-Letter Box an effective outlet for some of the negative feelings that are bound to accumulate in any family.

IMOK SIGNS[2]

Purpose

This activity helps everyone in the family to become aware of the "putdowns" and "killer-statements" that they use on each other, and which are so destructive to self-esteem. IMOK signs also teach family members to appreciate and put up with each other. This activity can have real impact on improving family relationships.

Instructions

For this activity each family member needs a 4 x 6

note card, a safety-pin, and a box of colored stars, e.g., blue and red stars. Tell your family the IMOK story below. Then, have each family member make an IMOK sign, by printing the letters I-M-O-K on the 4 x 6 note cards. Family members are then to attach the IMOK sign to their clothing with a safety-pin. Explain that each time someone in the family says or does something that makes him or her feel under par (less lovable and capable), that person is to put a red star on his or her sign, to indicate having felt "put down," etc. On the other hand, each time someone in the family does or says something to make another member feel better than par (more lovable and capable) the happy individual is to put a blue star on his or her sign, to indicate feeling built up.

At lunch time, hold a discussion of how things are going. Encourage each family member to voice his or her own discoveries of what puts people down and what builds them up. You might suggest that the family brainstorm some activities to do in the afternoons, to insure that by evening, everyone's sign is covered with a blue star, and that there are no red stars. The same kind of discussion can then be held at dinner time. Just before bedtime, ask your family to remove the IMOK signs, and to discuss what each member has learned about the way people like to be treated.

MY TIME

Purpose
   Children love this activity; it's a real ego booster.

Instructions

Set aside a short period of time each week (10-20 minutes), for each person in the family. This is that person's "my time." During this time, he or she can do whatever he or she wants (within reason, of course.) The person can lead the family in singing, in playing a game with someone of his or her choosing, can have the whole family's undivided attention, be left alone, or do whatever he or she wishes. And the rest of the family must try to cooperate.

Footnotes

[1]The idea for this activity comes from Karen Kinsler, and is gratefully acknowledged.
[2]The idea for this activity comes from Sid Simon's, *IALAC Story*, Argus, Niles, Ill., and is gratefully acknowledged.

16 SPECIAL TIME: SELF-ESTEEM ACTIVITIES TO PREPARE YOUR CHILD FOR A TV WORLD

SPECIAL TIME: SELF-ESTEEM ACTIVITIES TO PREPARE YOUR CHILD FOR A TV WORLD

In our family, my wife and I try to set aside some time each day, even if it is only five minutes, to spend with each child individually. Our chidren call this their "Special Time" with Mom or Dad. We use the time in many ways—to play games, to talk about things, to go places—but one of the favorite ways we use Special Time is to do self-esteem activities. Our children enjoy these activities very much, and best of all, the activities have had a significant effect upon our children's feelings of self-confidence and personal adequacy. The major goal of the activities is to help the children focus on their own positive qualities and abilities, so that they see themselves as worthwhile persons and can thus stand up to, and not cave in under, the pressure that TV and their peers exert. In addition, Special Time can greatly improve parent-child relationships in the family.

We hope that you will enjoy and find the following Special Time activities as useful with your children as we have with ours. To make the most of your child's Special Time, simply follow the instructions provided with each activity.

ME TREE

Purpose

This activity helps younger children to identify and reflect upon things they are good at doing, and thus serves to increase their feelings of self-esteem. For older children and adolescents, Me Tree serves the same purpose, by having them focus on their strengths and accomplishments.

Instructions

For Younger Children: Give your child a large sheet of paper and help him to draw the outline of a tree (see figure below). Write the child's name on the trunk of the tree. Then say, "Let's think about some of the things you are good at doing. Maybe you are good at dancing. You say what you think you are good at doing and I'll draw a picture of it, and write it on your Me Tree. This will be your special tree, to remind you of all the things you can do. Then, anytime that you get good at something new, you can put it on your Me Tree, until the whole tree is filled up. Now, what do you want to put on the tree?"

As your child tells you what to put on the tree, draw a symbol to represent the activity, and write the word underneath. For example, your child might say "swimming." Draw a stick figure swimming or a picture of a swimming pool, and write the word *swimming* underneath. If your child has trouble thinking of activities, help him out, but don't force him to put anything on the tree. For example, I suggested to my five-year-old daughter that she put down "a good drawer" on her tree. She flatly refused, saying, "Daddy! I can't draw!" She was willing to put painting on her tree, however. Thus, I realized that at age five, children have already developed some strong internal standards. My daughter knew what good drawing looked like, and she knew her drawing didn't look like that. But in the area of painting, she felt her paintings looked as good as some of the professional ones hanging in our house. I had to agree.

When your child is finished, hang the Me Tree on a wall for the whole family to admire. Family members can ask questions about the items on the Me Tree, or validate the child (for a discussion on how to validate, see page 233). It might be fun for each member of the family, including Mom and Dad, to make a Me Tree.

My five-year-old loved doing the Me Tree. She covered the branches of the tree with things like camping, building with blocks, making a snowman, turning a summersault, counting, and so on. Then, she could hardly wait to put something new on the tree. She decided that she would like to put tap dancing on the tree, so for the next two weeks she danced up a storm until she felt she was good enough to put it on the tree. Then, tap dancing went on the Me Tree. Perhaps my daughter "cheated" a bit, but by her standards she was pretty good at dancing and that was what counted. My daughter's Me Tree still hangs in our family room.

For Older Children: Have your child draw a tree with both branches and roots (see figure below). On the roots, the child is to write or draw as many of his/her strengths, talents, and abilities as he/she can think of. On the branches, the child is to write or draw as many personal accomplishments, successes, and achievements as he/she can think of. When you are both finished, share your Me Trees and compare notes. Validate each others strengths and achievements.

MY BOOK ABOUT ME

Purpose

Children often love to write their own books. This activity gives them a grown-up feeling. When the book is about their own feelings, it is even more special, and tells them non-verbally that their feelings and thoughts are very important. This serves to build their sense of self-worth and adequacy.

Instructions

Provide your child with a notebook, or place 20 or 30 sheets of paper between two pieces of colored construction paper and bind them together with string. On the cover, in bold letters, write the words, MY BOOK ABOUT ME. Then have your child sign his/her name on the cover and glue a picture of himself/herself on it. Explain that this is to be the child's very own special book about himself/herself that he/she will write in whenever he/she wants. Get your child started by placing one of the unfinished sentences below on each page. The task is to complete the sentence stem into a story about the child. Use some of the following sentence stems, or make up your own:

One of the happiest times in my life. . . .

A sad time in my life. . . .

My friends. . . .

My family. . . .

Something I'm proud of is. . . .

A dream I have is. . . .

Someday I will. . . .

I love. . . .

I hate. . . .

People make me feel good when they. . . .

ME COLLAGE

Purpose

Children often have difficulty identifying their strengths and abilities verbally. However, by looking through old magazines and seeing things that they are good at or enjoy, they can find many strengths and abilities.

Instructions

For Older Children: Provide your child with a large sheet of construction paper (newsprint, butcher paper, cardboard), magazines, colored magic markers, crayons, scissors, and glue. The task is to make a Me

Collage by cutting out and pasting pictures and words which represent the child's strengths, achievements, things he/she likes to do, people he/she admires, goals, values, and so on. When the Me Collage is finished, hang it on the wall for display.

This is a fun activity for the whole family. Family members can compare their similarities and differences.

For Younger Children: Have younger children make a collage which focuses on only one part of themselves. For example, they could make a collage of all the things they like to do (foods they like to eat, things they think are beautiful, ways they feel sometimes).

FAMILY COLLAGE

This is a variation on the Me Collage. Instead of each person doing his own separate collage, the whole family does a giant Family Collage. Include things like family achievements, family traditions, and family sayings, as well as more personal things about each family member.

STRENGTHS COLLAGE

This is another variation on the Me Collage. Instead of doing a personal collage, each family member chooses a partner and makes a collage which tells about the partner's strengths and good points. When everyone finishes, each person gets a turn to share his collage with his partner, with the rest of the family watching and listening.

PERSONAL SHIELD

Purpose

The Personal Shield is a fun way for children and adolescents to reflect upon their personal achievements, goals, and strengths. It serves to build feelings of self-worth and "I-canness."

Instructions

For Older Children: Instruct your child to draw a shield. See figure below. Then have the child do the following:

1. In the upper left-half corner, the child is to draw a picture of his/her greatest personal achievement.

2. In the upper right-hand corner, the child is to draw a picture of something that he/she would like to achieve.

3. In the lower left-hand corner, the child is to draw a picture of the greatest gift he/she has to offer others.

4. In the lower right-hand corner, the child is to draw a picture of the happiest moment in his/her life.

5. Underneath the shield, the child is to write a motto, or several words that he/she would like to be remembered by after death.

The child can then paint the Personal Shield with bright colors, and hang it on the wall for the whole family to admire and discuss.

For Younger Children: Have them draw only one or two things on their shields. For example, they might draw something they are good at, or a favorite recent experience.

FAMILY TREE

Purpose
This activity helps children develop pride in their family and in themselves by learning about their family's historical roots, talents, achievements, and contributions.

Instructions
For Older Children: The child's task is to do a Family Tree. For each person in the family (brothers and sisters, parents and grandparents, aunts and uncles), including himself, the child is to do a brief biographical sketch. Here are some questions the child might focus on:

1. What does/did this person look like? (Photographs can be used here if available.)

2. How does/did he/she make a living?

3. What are/were his/her talents, abilities, strengths?

4. What are/were his/her achievements, successes, contributions? (Awards, newspaper clippings, and pictures can be used here.)

5. What does/did he/she stand for, believe in, fight for? (Newspaper clippings, and pictures can be used here.)

The child can interview family members (brothers and sisters, aunts and uncles, grandparents and great-grandparents), or persons who know or once knew the subject to gather information. If the child is enthusiastic, the project can be expanded to include several generations. This makes a nice family project.

When the Family Tree is complete, the sketches can be displayed in a photo album, with one or two pages devoted to each family member.

ME BOX

Purpose

This activity helps children realize that they have two sides to themselves, a public side that others know, and a private, inner self that only they know. The Me Box teaches children that they can control and keep private their inner self, or share it with someone special, if they wish. Children love knowing they have this control, and enjoy sharing the inside of their Me Box with others of their choosing. The Me Box is a great self-esteem booster.

Instructions

For Older Children: Ask your child to find a box with a cover or lid. The box should be at least as large as a shoe box, and preferably larger. On the outside of the box, the child is to cut and paste pictures, words, or symbols, or attach objects which represent the things that he/she likes, is good at, feels strongly about, and so on. This is the child's public self—the self that others know. On the inside of the box, the child is to paste pictures or place objects which represent a more private and intimate self—the side of the child which most others do not know about. This might include thoughts and feelings, crisis points and turning points in his/her life, objects of special importance, poems and sayings which have special meaning, and so on.

Tell the child that the Me Box is personal, and that no one is allowed to look in it unless the child invites them to do so. Even then, the child can decide what to share and what to keep private.

For Younger Children: Younger children can decorate the inside and outside of their Me Boxes with pictures and words which represent the things they like to do, places they like to go, foods they like to eat, favorite animals, and so on.

ME CHART

Purpose

This activity gives each child in the family the

spotlight for a week. It is an enjoyable way to remind children that they are special persons who are appreciated.

Instructions

For this activity you will need a magic marker and a large sheet of paper (large enough to trace the outline of your child's whole body). Have your child lie in any position he or she wishes on the large sheet of paper, and trace the outline of his/her body with the magic marker. Write the child's name and the date in one of the corners. Then, do one of the following:

1. Have each family member write what they appreciate most about the child on the Me Chart and sign their name. For example: "I appreciate the friendly way you treat me," signed Mary. Nothing negative should be written on the Me Chart.

2. Have each family member make a list of the child's best points and sign his name.

3. Have the child record the high points of each day for a week and keep an emotional barometer of feelings.

4. Have the child make a self-portrait by drawing and painting in his or her body outline.

If you have several children in the family, feature one child each week; that way, each child will have his or her chance to shine.

HIGH POINTS AND LOW POINTS

Purpose

Having children identify and reflect on the high and low points of their lives often serves to remind them of their successes, accomplishments, and achievements, as well as the fact that they had the strength and fortitude to weather and outlast their low points.

Instructions

Have your child draw a line on a sheet of paper. At one end of the line, the child is to write the date of his/her birth and the word *birth*. At the other end of the line, the child is to write the word *present*. Then, the child is to start at one end of the line and identify both the high points and low points in his/her life. (The task can be limited by having the child identify a certain number of high and low points—five high points and five low points, for example.) The child should indicate high points by drawing an arrow up from the line at about the point on the line when the event occurred. Conversely, he/she is to draw an arrow down from the line to indicate low points. (The length of the arrows can indicate the relative highs and lows of each event—if you wish to add this variation.) Key words to indicate the nature of the event and the approximate date that the event occurred should be written over and under the arrows.

Then, have your child discuss his or her high and low points with you, or with the rest of the family. The low points often bring back negative feelings, which can have a detrimental effect upon the child's self-image, unless you help the child to realize that he/she is indeed a strong person for having weathered and passed through those low points. Often, this recognition can have a positive effect upon the child's feling of "I-canness." However, if you feel that the low points may have more of a negative effect than a positive effect on your child, do only the high points activity.

Another variation is to have the child indicate the turning points in his or her life by placing an X on the line and noting, above or below the line, the nature of the event and the date that the event occurred. Many times, the child's high and low points will also be turning points. A turning point may be defined as "an event in the child's life, which if it had not occurred, would have made the child a different person than the child is today."

Try doing a high and low points line yourself. Your child will enjoy and appreciate getting to see a bit of your life-history as well.

FUZZIES

Purpose

Self-esteem is a two-way street. The child must learn to esteem others as well as to esteem himself or herself. If children are taught to respect and appreciate others, this often serves three goals. One, giving makes the child feel good and important. Two, giving helps to nurture the receiver's self-esteem. And three, the receiver is very likely to return the appreciation to the giver, thus serving to nurture his or her self-esteem. Fuzzies teaches this important and valuable lesson.

Instructions
    Read your child the Fuzzy story below. Then, have him/her answer the following questions.

1. What are Fuzzies? What are Pricklies?

2. How do you give people Fuzzies? Pricklies?

3. Would you rather get Fuzzies or Pricklies? Why?

A FUZZY STORY[1]

Once upon a time, not too long ago, there lived a very kind and gentle king who ruled over a tiny kingdom. The people in the kingdom loved their king, and they loved each other. In fact, all persons carried a bag of Fuzzies over their shoulders. Whenever they would meet each other, they would reach into their bag and pull out a Fuzzy. "Here, have a Fuzzy," they would say to each other.

The Fuzzies would snuggle up and make the people feel good for the rest of the day. The people in this tiny kingdom gave out their Fuzzies freely, because they liked making each other happy.

One day, the kind and gentle king called his people together and announced that he was taking a very long trip to another land to see how people there lived. His brother, Prince Klutz, would rule as king until the real king's return.

Now, Prince Klutz was the only person in the whole kingdom that really didn't like to give Fuzzies. He was greedy and wanted the Fuzzies all to himself. Several days after the kind and gentle king had departed, Prince Klutz decided upon a plan to get everyone in the kingdom to give him all of their Fuzzies.

Now, Prince Klutz knew that he couldn't come right out and make a law against giving out Fuzzies, because the people just wouldn't stand for it. So he decided upon another plan. He called all the people in the kingdom together. After much Fuzzy-giving, Prince Klutz called the gathering to order. In a very serious voice, he announced that the kingdom was in trouble. There would soon be a shortage of Fuzzies, if people didn't stop giving them away so freely.

The people were very sad to hear this, for they loved getting and giving Fuzzies. The prince told them that from now on they could only give Fuzzies on special days, like Christmas, Valentine's Day, Mother's Day, Father's Day, and birthdays. The rest of the time, people were to give each other Pricklies.

Now, the people disliked Pricklies. But they agreed. The prince collected all the Fuzzy bags and gave everyone a Prickly bag instead. Now, each time the people in the kingdom met one another, they would say, "Here, have a Prickly."

Soon people in the kingdom stopped smiling. They would go out of their way to avoid each other. Nobody went visiting anymore. Instead, people stayed home and kept their doors locked. It was a very unhappy kingdom. The only things that people looked forward to were the special days, like Christmas and Valentine's Day and birthdays, when they could once again give Fuzzies.

Now, there lived in the kingdom a young woman who was very upset by all this. So she decided to go in search of the kind and gentle king. When the young woman found the king, in the far and distant land, she told the king about what had happened.

The king was very upset. For only he knew that the Fuzzies would never run out; when one Fuzzy was taken from the Fuzzy bag, another would automatically take its place. Of course, he would have to return to his kingdom to get things straightened out.

When the king returned home, he called all of his people together and told them the truth. The people cheered and were very glad. As soon as they had their Fuzzy bags back, they began giving Fuzzies to each other as fast as they could.

> The king was happy because now his people could never be fooled again. Prince Klutz was happy because he could still have all the Fuzzies he wanted without ever running out. And the people were happy because never again would they have to give Pricklies.

As a follow-up, have your child make some Fuzzies to give other people. Here are some suggestions:

1. Make a Fuzzy card. Draw pictures of Fuzzies on the card, or make them out of yarn, etc., and glue them on. Write something like, "Here's a Fuzzy specially made for you; it comes with lots of love, and hugs and kisses, too."

2. Make a little Fuzzy from yarn or soft material. Tie a sign around its neck reading, "A Fuzzy just for you!"

3. Make a Fuzzies Box and put Fuzzies in it. People can reach in the box and pull out a Fuzzy.

ADDITIONAL ACTIVITIES *

The following activities help to develop and nurture children's self-esteem.

1. Have your child complete the sentence stem, "I'm special because. . . ." several times. Then tell your child why you think he or she is special.

2. Ask your child to draw or paint a self-portrait. Hang the portrait where the entire family can see it.

3. Have your child keep a list of the "good deeds" he or she has done for others.

4. Have your child make a scrapbook about himself or herself. The child is to fill the scrapbook with photos, writing, letters, newspaper clippings, and other mementos that have special meaning to the child.

5. Ask your child to tell you what he or she likes best about each part of his or her body; e.g., nose, eyes, hair, hands, and so on.

6. Have your child complete the sentence stem "(Name) likes me because I. . . ." several times.

7. Have your child design a poster or button which points out his/her strengths and talents.

8. Ask your child to write a resume of his/her experiences, achievements, successes, and skills.

9. Make a suggestion box, and encourage family members to put in the box suggestions on how family members can support and care for each other more effectively.

10. Put up a bulletin board on which family members can post notices of things they need help with, etc. Call it the I NEED BOARD.

11. Have your child make a list of all his or her strengths.

12. Teach your child to ask for attention when he or she needs it. This is very effective for young children, and can cut down on their practice of attention-getting behavior, which often serves to annoy the parent instead of getting the child the positive attention that he is seeking.

13. Have your child complete the sentence, "I used to _____ but now I'm _____."

14. Help your child make a list of put-down and "killer" statements that people use to make each other feel bad. Discuss why people feel a need to use hurtful words with each other, and what can be done to deal with the problem.

15. Have your child complete the sentence, "I'm proud that I. . . ."

16. Have your child make a list of "I Can" statements. The list should contain all the things your child can do, e.g., "I can tie my own shoes."

17. Hold a family "bragging" session, in which family members "brag" about each other's strengths, abilities, achievements, and successes.

18. Give your child a mirror and ask the child to say to the mirror, "Mirror, Mirror, tell me what you see; tell me what you think is best in me." The child is to pretend that the mirror answers, and to report the mirror's response.

19. Have your child write a letter to himself or herself expressing appreciation for who he/she is and what

he/she has done with his/her life.

20. Have your child complete the sentence, "I'm a success because. . . ."

21. Have your child list any special names and endearment words or phrases that loved ones or friends have used with him/her. Then encourage your child to discuss his/her feelings about each name or endearment.

22. Have your child write something he or she would like to get rid of on a sheet of paper, and then wad up the paper and throw it in the trash can. Then have the child discuss his/her feelings. Help the child deal with the problem but don't try to solve it for the child, as this can often make him/her feel worse about himself/herself instead of better.

23. Have your child make a list of all the things that are special to him/her. Have the child discuss her list with you.

24. Have your child complete the sentence, "My favorite place is _____." Then, encourage the child to share why this is a favorite place.

25. Trace your child's name on colored contact paper in large letters, and post the paper in the child's room. Tell the child why you think his/her name is special.

Footnotes

[1] I have tried to trace the original source of the several Fuzzy stories I've heard, but to date I have been unable to do so. This is my own version of this enjoyable fairy tale.

SELECTED ANNOTATED BIBLIOGRAPHY

* *Children and Television* by Gerald S. Lesser (Vintage).
  The inside story of *Sesame Street*.

* *Children, The Challenge* by Rudolph Dreikurs (Hawthorne).
  This book explores practical ways to approach childrearing discipline. Dreikurs expounds his famous method of "natural and logical consequences."

* *Helping Your Child Learn Right From Wrong: A Guide to Values Clarification* by Sid Simon and Sally Olds (Simon & Schuster).
  A parents' book outlining a way to help children learn a process for arriving at their own values. Many values-clarification strategies with a family focus.

* *I Am Lovable And Capable* by Sidney Simon (Argus).
  A pamphlet with a detailed version of the famous IALAC story, demonstrating how a child's self-concept is so easily diminished in a typical day.

* *Parent Effectiveness Training* by Thomas Gordon (Wyden).
  Dr. Gordon's famous work in establishing "win-win" situations in family relationships is skillfully presented in this book.

* *Personalizing Education: Values Clarification and Beyond* by Leland and Mary Martha Howe (Hart).
  A handbook of practical ways to make values clarification and other effective techniques an integral part of the classroom. Over 100 strategies, worksheets, and sample units.

* *The Plug-In Drug* by Marie Winn (Viking).
  Examines the effects of television on children and the family.

* *Remote Control* by Frank Mankiewicz and Joel Swerdlow (Times Books).
  The most comprehensive study available of the effects of television on our children, family, and society.

* *Taking Charge of Your Life* by Leland Howe (Argus).
  This is a series of activities designed to help you to take charge of your life and to achieve your goals. This book is useful for parents to help children to take responsibility for their lives.

* *Values Clarification: A Handbook of Practical Strategies* by Sidney Simon, Leland Howe, and Howard Kirschenbaum (Hart).
  Detailed instructions for 70 values-clarification strategies, with many examples for the basic

strategies. An invaluable handbook for parents and teachers.

* *100 Ways to Enhance Self Concept* by Jack Canfield and H. Wells (Prentice-Hall).
Ideas and exercises to help children of all ages feel better about themselves.

If you are interested in having your name placed on our mailing list to receive notification of workshops, new books, and other materials related to raising children in a TV world, send your name, address and zip code to:

TV World
PHEC
8504 Germantown Ave.
Phila., Pa. 19118

INDEX

ABC network
    Address, 82
ACT
    See ACTION FOR CHILDREN'S TELEVISION
Action for Children's Television, 84, 163
Activities
    Instead of TV, 26, 27, 36, 59-65, 136-145
    Self-esteem, 235-254
    Using TV, 93-111, 120-135, 163-173, 178, 179
    Values-clarification, 191-231
    See also individual names
Addiction
    To TV 55-65
Advertising
    See COMMERCIALS
Aggression
    See VIOLENCE
All in the Family, 165
Association for Childhood
    Education International, 22 (footnote)
American Medical Association, 41
Attitude
    Influencing children's, toward TV, 27-37

Barbie Dolls, 135
Baseball or a Surprise Party?
    Values dilemma, 207, 208
Bewitched, 160
Black Beauty, 101
Books
    About television, 10
Brady Bunch, The, 123, 165
Brady, Marsha, 123
Broken promise
    Values dilemma, 207

Canfield, Jack, 259
Cartoons, TV, 42, 44
Cassettes, audio
    How to use to increase learning, 106-109
    Use in the classroom, 171

CBS network
   Address, 82
Chachi, 123
Chicago Prime Time School Television, 12, 91, 159, 168
Child-rearing
   Approaches, 115-120
Children
   Activities for, *see* ACTIVITIES *and individual names*
   Alternatives to TV for, 26, 27; 55-65
   Hours spent watching TV, 9, 177
   How to regulate TV time for, 30-37; 55-65
   TV-related emotional upsets, 69-74
Children and TV, 22 (footnote), 92 (footnote)
Children, the Challenge, 36, 257
Children's Day
   Values-clarification activity, 227, 228
Chronicle, The, 165
Classroom
   See SCHOOLS
Closer Look at Our Schools, A, 132
Coca-Cola, 53
Collages, 136, 239-241
Comic Books, 98-101
Commercials
   Advertising techniques, 52-54
   Brainwashing, 10, 52-54, 115, 183, 185, 186
   Cost, 19, 49
   How to combat, 49-54, 83, 92
   How to teach children to make, 106
   How to use breaks for activities, 121, 122
   Learning from 97, 101, 102, 104
   Stereotyping, 166, 167
Complaints
   How to make, about TV, 79-85
Constitution, U.S., 183
Consumer-reporter, 108
Corporation for Public Broadcasting
   Address, 82
Creative Play Things, 50

Dead-Letter Box
   Values-clarification activity, 228, 229
"Dear Abby" Time
   Values-clarification activity, 205, 206
Demographics
   How to use TV to teach, 104
Department of Agriculture, 108

Dinner Table Reflections
    Values-clarification activity, 225, 226
Disney World, 203
Divorce
    Topic for family discussion time, 212
Documentaries, 96, 107, 124, 125, 169, 184
Dramatics
    How to use TV to teach, 105
Dreikurs, Rudolf, 36, 257
Drew, Nancy, 101
Duska, Ronald, 145, (footnote)

Ecology vs. Unemployment
    Values dilemma, 208, 209
Educators
    Use of TV, 12, 159-173
Effectiveness Training
    Address, 154
    See also PARENT EFFECTIVENESS TRAINING
Eight Is Enough, 165
Eleanor and Franklin, 163
Emotional upsets
    TV-related, 69-74, 95, 149, 150
Environment
    Topic for family discussion time, 215
Executive producer, 80, 81

Family
    Alternatives to TV, 61-65
    Centered-time, 30
    Meetings on TV violence, 43-45
    Special time activities, 235-254
    Time, values activities for, 191-231
    Topic for family discussion time, 210
Family Auction
    Values-clarification activity, 202-204
Family Coat of Arms
    Values-clarification activity, 204
Family Circle Time
    Values-clarification activity, 195-199
Family Collage
    Self-esteem activity, 240
Family Discussion Time
    Values-clarification activity, 209-217
Family Feud, 110, 165
Family Guests
    Values-clarification activity, 181

Family Interview Time
    Values-clarification activity, 199-201
Family Mailbox
    Values-clarification activity, 224-225
Family Secret Pal
    Values-clarification activity, 293, 294
Family Tree
    Self-esteem activity, 242-243
Family validations
    Values-clarification activity, 292, 293
Family Values Dilemmas
    Values-clarification activity, 206-209
FCC
    See FEDERAL COMMUNICATIONS COMMISSION
Federal Communications Commission, 19, 83
Finders Keepers
    Values dilemma, 207
Fisher-Price, 50
Focusing
    During Family Circle Time, 196
Fonzie, 123
Fordwick, the Reverend, 165
Forest Service, 107
Friends
    Topic for family discussion time, 210, 211
Fuzzies
    Self-esteem activity, 247-251

Game Shows, 109-111
Goal chart 61-63
Good Times, 165
Gordon, Thomas, 74, 75 (footnote), 153, 257
Government
    Debates about TV, 10
    Regulation of TV, 85

Happy Days, 123, 165
Hardy Boys, The, 101
Harmon, Merrill, 145 (footnote)
Health
    Topic for family discussion time, 215
Helping Your Child Learn Right From Wrong, 128, 257
High Points and Low Points
    Self-esteem activity, 246, 247
Hitler, Adolf, 165
Hollywood Squares, 110, 111
Hot Wheels Racing Car, 135
Howe, Leland, 127, 136, 145 (footnote), 258

Howe, Mary Martha, 105 (footnote), 136, 258
Human Side of Human Beings, The, 75 (footnote)

IALAC Story, 231 (footnote), 257
I Am Lovable and Capable, 257
IMOK Signs
    Values-clarification activities, 229, 230
Ingalls Family, 122
Interview
    How to conduct a TV, 108, 109

Jackins, Harvey, 75 (footnote)
James at 16, 125
Jeffersons, The, 165
Johnson, Lyndon B., 19

King, Martin Luther, 124, 125
Kinsler, Karen, 231 (footnote)
Kirschenbaum, Howard, 127, 136, 145 (footnote), 258

Laissez-faire
    Approach to child-rearing, 115-117
Land of the Lost, 178
Lassie, 69, 72, 73
Laws
    Topic for family discussion time, 215
Learning
    Effect of TV on, 19, 91
    Using TV to increase 93-111, 159-173
Leisure Time
    Topic for family discussion time, 215
Lesser, Gerald S., 92 (footnote), 257
Little House on the Prairie, The, 26, 36, 94, 95, 101, 165
Logical Consequences, 31-36
Love
    Topic for family discussion time, 211, 212

Malcolm X, 125
Mankiewicz, Frank, 10, 20, 22 (footnote), 92 (footnote), 179 (footnote), 258
Marcase, Michael, 160, 162, 163
March of Dimes, 107
Marriage
    Topic for family discussion time, 212
Match Game, 110
Math
    How to use TV to improve, 101-104

McAndrew, Michael, 160
Me Box
    Self-esteem activity, 243, 244
Me Chart
    Self-esteem activity, 244, 245
Me Collage
    Self-esteem activity, 239, 240
Me Tree
    Self-esteem activity, 236-238
Media
    Debates about TV, 10
Mister Rodgers Neighborhood, 12, 25, 26
Mein Kampf, 165
Money
    Topic for family discussion time, 212, 213
Moral Development
    Influence of TV on 115-145
Moral Development: *A Guide to Piaget and Kohlberg*, 145
Moralizing
    Approach to child-rearing, 118, 119
Moral Judgments
    Topic for family discussion time, 213
Mount Vernon, N.Y.
    Use of Philadelphia Project, 161
My Book About Me
    Self-esteem activity, 238, 239
My Time
    Values-clarification activity, 230-231

Name that Tune, 110
National Child Research Center, 19
National Commission on the Causes and Prevention of Violence, 19
National Dairy Council, 107
National Education Association, 163
National Parent-Teacher Association, 41
Natural Consequences, 31-33
NBC Network
    Address, 82
Newlywed Game, The, 110
Newspaper
    How to use in children's news programs, 106-109
    Reviews of TV shows, 94, 95
    Television page, 93, 102, 103
    TV scripts printed in, 163
    Values issues in, 138, 139
Newsweek, 22 (footnote), 45 (footnote), 49, 54 (footnote), 91, 92 (footnote)
No-lose problem solving, 28

Olds, Sally Wendkos, 145 (footnote), 257
On Becoming a Person, 75 (footnote)
One Day at a Time, 165
One-Hundred Twenty-Eight Thousand Dollar Question, The, 110
One Hundred Ways to Enhance Self Concept, 259
Our Favorite Things
    Values-clarification activity, 220

Parents
    Action for children's television, 84
    Effect on children's TV viewing, 12, 13, 91
Passivity
    Fostered by TV, 19, 57
Parent Effectiveness Training, 153, 154
Parent Effectiveness Training, 74, 75 (footnote), 153, 154, 257
Personal Shield
    Self-esteem activity, 241-242
Personal tastes
    Topic for family discussion time, 213
Personalizing Education: Values Clarification and Beyond, 136, 257
PET
    See PARENT EFFECTIVENESS TRAINING
Philadelphia
    Quiz shows shown in, 110
Philadelphia Schools' Reading Project, 12, 91, 160-163,
    164, 168, 170 (address)
Playskool, 50
Plug-In Drug, The: Television, Children, and the Family,
    10, 20, 57, 65, (footnote), 184, 258
Politics
    Topic for family discussion time 213, 214
Price is Right, The, 110
Pricklies, 248-251
Prime-Time School TV
    Address, 168
    See also CHICAGO PRIME-TIME SCHOOL TELEVISION
Prince Klutz, 249
Problem-solving, 28-36, 206-209
Programming, 79-85, 96, 97, 104, 109, 110, 115, 171, 184
PTA
    See NATIONAL PARENT-TEACHER ASSOCIATION
PTST
    See PRIME-TIME SCHOOL TV
Public Television, 82, 104

Questions
    Raised by TV, 149-158
Quiz shows, 109-111

Race
    Topic for family discussion time, 214
Raths, Louis, 145 (footnote)
Ratings, TV, 79
Reading Show, The, 162, 163, 172, 173
Reflective Listening, 150-158, 197
Reform
    Television 19, 41, 49, 79-85, 184
Reading
    Effect of TV on scores, 11
    How to use TV to improve, 93-101
    TV used to improve skills, 12, 91, 159-163
Regulation
    Of TV programming, 85
    Of TV viewing, 25, 26, 58-65
Religion
    Topic for family discussion time, 214
Remote Control: Television and the Manipulation of American Life, 10, 11,
    20, 22 (footnote), 45, 92 (footnote), 179 (footnote), 183, 184, 258
Reruns, 109, 110
Rodgers, Carl, 75 (footnote)
Rookies, The, 160
Rules and regulations
    Topic for family discussion time, 215

Safety
    Topic for family discussion time, 215
Sanford and Son, 95, 160
Scavenger hunt, 139, 140
    See also VALIDATION SCAVENGER HUNT
School
    Topic for family discussion time, 215, 216
Science
    How to use TV to teach, 105
Schools
    How to use television in, 159-173
    Using educational television, 91
Scripts
    How to use, 168-170
    The Reading Show, or The Vanishing Shadow, 172, 173
    Used in classroom, 160-161
    Used on educational TV, 162, 163
Self esteem
    Activities 233-254
Selma, Alabama, 124
Sesame Street, 91, 169, 257
Sex
    Dialogue between mother and daughter on, 151-153

Topic for family discussion time, 211, 212
Shaw, George Bernard, 94
Simon, Sidney B., 127, 128, 136, 145 (footnote), 165, 231 (footnote), 257, 258
Solomon, Bernard, 85 (footnote), 160, 170
Speaking out activities, 143-145
Stereotyping
    On TV, 166, 167
Strengths Collage
    Self-esteem activity, 240-241
Studies
    Of moral development, 116-117
    Of TV and effects, 19, 41, 91, 161, 183
Supreme Court, 183
Swerdlow, Joel, 10, 20, 22 (footnote), 92 (footnote), 179 (footnote), 258
Taking Charge of Your Life, 258
Taking inventory
    Values-clarification activity, 216-219
Tandem Productions, 81
Tattle Tales, 110
Technology
    And TV, 171
Teenagers
    Hours spent watching TV, 9
    How to regulate TV time for, 30, 31
Television
    Addiction, 55-65
    As babysitter, 26, 37, 91, 177-179
    Debate about, 10, 41
    Educational, 12, 91, 159-173
    Effect on children and families, 9-13, 19-22, 41-45, 91, 115-145, 183, 184
    Hours spent watching by young persons, 9
    How to use in the classroom, 159-173
    Influence on moral development, 115-145
    Location of set, 65
    Networks, 79-85
    Programs, 12, 25, 26, 35, 36, 69, 72, 73, 79-85, 91, 95-97, 101, 109, 110, 115, 122, 123, 124, 125, 160, 162, 163, 165, 166, 167, 168, 169
    Questions raised by, and how to answer, 149-158
    Reform, 19, 41, 49, 79-85, 184
    Regulating children's viewing, 25-37, 41-45
    Studies of effects, 19, 41, 91, 183
    Violence 9, 10, 41-45
    See also COMMERCIALS *and individual shows*
Television Information Office, The, 83, 84
Television Reading Program, 160, 170 (address)
    See also PHILADELPHIA SCHOOLS' READING PROJECT
Telling Tales
    Values dilemma, 208

Time
    "Dear Abby," 205, 206
    Family, activities for, 191-231
    Family-centered, 30
    Family circle, 195-199
    Family discussion, 209
    Family interview, 199-201
    Special, self-esteem activities for, 235-254
    Spent by children and teenagers watching TV, 9, 31, 177
    TV, used to improve learning skills 93-111, 159-173, 177-179
To Pull or Not to Pull the Plug
    Values dilemma, 208
To Tell the Truth, 110
Toys, 19, 49, 50, 51, 53, 135, 194
TV Guide, 103
TV World
    Address, 259
Twenty-five Thousand Dollar Pyramid, 110

UHF, 82, 83, 104
Universal Studio, 81

Validation Scavenger Hunt
    Values-clarification activity, 227
Values
    How children develop, 116, 117
    Influence of TV on, 115
    See also MORAL DEVELOPMENT, VALUE CLARIFICATION
Values and Teaching, 145 (footnote)
Values-clarification
    Activities, for family time, 191-231
    Activities, using TV, 120-145, 165
    Approach to child-rearing, 119, 120
Values Clarification: A Handbook, 136, 145 (footnote), 258
Values diary, 140
Values ranking, 128-133
Values stems
    Values-clarification activity, 221, 222
Values voting, 133-135, 192-195
Vanishing Shadow, The, 162, 172, 173
VHF, 83
Videotape, 160, 168, 169, 171
Violence
    TV, 9, 10, 13, 41-45

Walters, Harry F., 22 (footnote), 45 (footnote), 54 (footnote), 92 (footnote)
Walton
    Grandma, 165
    John-Boy, 165
Waltons, The, 26, 165
Warner Brothers Studio, 81
Weather, 107, 108
Wells, H. 259
"What TV does to kids," 22 (footnote), 45 (footnote),
    54 (footnote), 91, 92 (footnote)
Wheelan, Mariellen, 145 (footnote)
Welfare
    Topic for family discussion time, 216
Whobody Likes
    Values-clarification activity, 192-195
Winn, Marie, 10, 20, 57, 65 (footnote), 258
Women, rights and roles
    Topic for family discussion time, 216, 217
Writing
    How to use TV to improve, 105

Zoom, 26, 35